Confucius in East Asia

Confucianism's History in China, Korea, Japan, and Việt Nam

Second Edition

Front Cover: Statue of Confucius.

Back Cover: A stamp printed in China showing Confucius with his students, commemorating the 2540th anniversary of Confucius' birth, circa 1989.

Key Issues in Asian Studies, No. 13

AAS Resources for Teaching About Asia

CONFUCIUS IN EAST ASIA

CONFUCIANISM'S HISTORY IN CHINA, KOREA, JAPAN, AND VIỆT NAM

SECOND EDITION

JEFFREY L. RICHEY

Association for Asian Studies, Inc.
825 Victors Way, Suite 310
Ann Arbor, MI 48108 USA
www.asianstudies.org

KEY ISSUES IN ASIAN STUDIES

A series edited by Lucien Ellington, University of Tennessee at Chattanooga

"Key Issues" volumes complement the Association for Asian Studies' teaching journal, *Education About Asia*—a practical teaching resource for secondary school, college, and university instructors, as well as an invaluable source of information for students, scholars, libraries, and those who have an interest in Asia.

Formed in 1941, the Association for Asian Studies (AAS)—the largest society of its kind, with over 5,500 members worldwide—is a scholarly, non-political, non-profit professional association open to all persons interested in Asia.

For further information, please visit www.asianstudies.org

AAS books are distributed by Columbia University Press.

For orders or inquiries, please visit https://cup.columbia.edu

Cataloging-in-Publication Data is available from the Library of Congress.

To Kelly, Nathan, and Colin

About "Key Issues in Asian Studies"

Key Issues in Asian Studies (*KIAS*) volumes engage major cultural and historical themes in the Asian experience. *Key Issues* books complement the Association for Asian Studies' teaching journal, *Education About Asia*, and serve as vital educational materials that are both accessible and affordable for classroom use.

Key Issues books tackle broad subjects or major events in an introductory but compelling style appropriate for survey courses. This series is intended for teachers and undergraduates at two- and four-year colleges as well as advanced high school students and secondary school teachers engaged in teaching Asian studies in a comparative framework and anyone with an interest in Asia.

For further information visit www.asianstudies.org.

Prospective authors interested in *Key Issues in Asian Studies* or *Education About Asia* are encouraged to contact Lucien Ellington: Lucien-Ellington@utc.edu.

"Key Issues" volumes available from AAS:

- *Shintō in the History and Culture of Japan* / Ronald S. Green
- *Indonesia: History, Heritage, Culture* / Kathleen M. Adams
- *The Philippines: From Earliest Times to the Present* / Damon L. Woods
- *Chinese Literature: An Introduction* / Ihor Pidhainy
- *The Mongol Empire in World History* / Helen Hundley
- *Japanese Literature: From Murasaki to Murakami* / Marvin Marcus
- *Japan Since 1945* / Paul E. Dunscomb
- *East Asian Societies* / W. Lawrence Neuman
- *Confucius in East Asia* / Jeffrey L. Richey
- *The Story of Việt Nam: From Prehistory to the Present* / Shelton Woods
- *Modern Chinese History* / David Kenley
- *Korea in World History* / Donald N. Clark
- *Traditional China in Asian and World History* / Tansen Sen & Victor Mair
- *Zen Past and Present* / Eric Cunningham
- *Japan and Imperialism, 1853–1945* / James L. Huffman
- *Japanese Popular Culture and Globalization* / William M. Tsutsui
- *Global India ca 100 CE: South Asia in Early World History* / Richard H. Davis
- *Caste in India* / Diane Mines
- *Understanding East Asia's Economic "Miracles"* / Zhiqun Zhu
- *Political Rights in Post-Mao China* / Merle Goldman
- *Gender, Sexuality, and Body Politics in Modern Asia* / Michael Peletz

About the Author

JEFFREY L. RICHEY is Professor of Asian Studies at Berea College. A graduate of the University of North Carolina at Greensboro, he completed graduate studies in East Asian religious history at Harvard University and the University of California at Berkeley before earning his Ph.D. in Cultural and Historical Studies of Religions with a concentration in East Asian religions at the Graduate Theological Union. He has edited and contributed to several  books on Confucian and other East Asian traditions, including *Teaching Confucianism* (New York: Oxford University Press, 2008), *The Patheos Guide to Confucianism* (Denver: Patheos Press, 2012), *The Sage Returns: Confucian Revival in Contemporary China* (Albany: SUNY Press, 2015), and *Daoism in Japan: Chinese Traditions and Their Influence on Japanese Religious Culture* (London and New York: Routledge, 2015). Dr. Richey's articles appear in numerous journals, including *Education About Asia, Journal of the Economic and Social History of the Orient, Numen, Religions, Religious Studies Review, Sino-Platonic Papers*, and *Teaching Theology and Religion*, as well as various anthologies, edited volumes, and encyclopedias, and he served as the founding Chinese Philosophy Area Editor for the *Internet Encyclopedia of Philosophy*. He remains deeply interested in East Asian traditions and their expressions in both premodern and contemporary East Asia, particularly cinema.

Contents

ILLUSTRATIONS

Figures

Maps

Acknowledgments

I am grateful to my Berea College colleagues Rebecca Bates, Chad Berry, Robert Foster, Phyllis Gabbard, Robert Hoag, Jeff Pool, and Patty Tarter for their invaluable support during the difficult period in which this work was in progress. The two anonymous reviewers of the manuscript provided many helpful suggestions and useful corrections. Lucien Ellington and Jonathan Wilson proved themselves to be extraordinarily patient and encouraging while still maintaining the high standards for which the *Key Issues in Asian Studies* series already is well known. Truly, this contribution to the series would not exist without their critical involvement. Finally, I wish to acknowledge the debt of gratitude that I owe to my students at Berea College, who have tested and shaped my understanding of Confucian traditions for over a decade now.

NOTE REGARDING THE SECOND EDITION (2022)

Scholars' publications rarely become popular enough to warrant updated editions, so I am very appreciative of my editor Lucien Ellington's suggestion that this slim volume be revisited and revised. Having now taught and written about Confucian and other East Asian traditions for more than twenty years, I remain thankful to my family, teachers, colleagues, students, and readers, all of whom have helped refine my understanding of Confucian traditions and many of whom have modeled Confucian virtue for me.

EDITOR'S INTRODUCTION

Most of us who study cultures that early China profoundly affected believe that, other important belief systems notwithstanding, Confucianism has exerted perhaps the most general influence on both ordinary people and many government officials in all such societies. In *Confucius in East Asia: Confucianism's History in China, Korea, Japan, and Việt Nam*, Jeff Richey told the story of the origins and evolution of Confucianism in each of these cultures in an engaging, accurate, and balanced manner. It is again my pleasure to write this introduction for Jeff's revised and updated edition following his highly successful first edition.

This should be no surprise to anyone who has worked with Jeff extensively. He is passionate, highly competent, and creative as both a scholar and teacher. Throughout the years, Jeff has published eight articles, essays, and reviews in *Education About Asia* on a wide variety of topics and on numerous occasions served as an external referee. Since the publication of the first edition of *Confucius in East Asia* in 2013, Jeff also encouraged and advised his Berea College colleague, Professor Lauren McKee, in the development of her forthcoming Key Issues volume, *Japanese Politics and Government*. This makes Berea College the only institution of higher learning where two faculty members have published Key Issues volumes for AAS. This should come as no surprise for readers who are familiar with Berea College's success in providing liberal arts education for students with limited economic resources while retaining outstanding faculty scholars and teachers.

In this revised and updated edition of *Confucius in East Asia*, Jeff provides an excellent historical overview of each culture and as impressively clearly depicts how ordinary people and elites in each society interpreted the teaching of Confucius and the Confucian canon, through a process that included already existing indigenous and foreign influences. Jeff manages to fit his depiction of each culture's Confucian experiences into a common organizational framework, which makes similarities and differences in the impact of Confucianism on different East Asian polities even more illuminating for the reader. In each treatment of a different culture, Jeff also does an excellent job of taking the reader from antiquity to the present. I am confident that this revised volume will be even more useful than the first volume to a wide array of audiences and academic areas.

As is always the case, the successful development of this volume would have been impossible without the help of several people. Sarah Schneewind read the initial proposal and Kevin Cunningham and Ronnie Littlejohn served as external referees. Special thanks also go to Kitt McAuliffe, who as a University of Tennessee at Chattanooga honors student provided invaluable comments on various chapters of the original manuscript.

Finally, I am deeply grateful to Jonathan Wilson, AAS Publications Manager, and to the AAS Editorial Board, and especially Bill Tsutsui, its chair, for their strong support of pedagogical initiatives such as Education About Asia and Key Issues in Asian Studies.

Lucien Ellington Series Editor, *Key Issues in Asian Studies*

TIMELINE

BCE

1046	Western Zhou dynasty begins (China)
551	Birth of Confucius (China)
221–206	Qin dynasty (China)
202	Han dynasty begins (China)
100s	Confucianism acquires state support in China, Korea, and Việt Nam

CE

100s	Buddhism and Daoism spread across East Asia
220	Han dynasty ends, period of disunity begins (China)
285	Traditional date of Confucianism's introduction to Japan
372	Confucian academy established in Korea
604	Prince Shōtoku's Seventeen-Article Constitution (Japan)
618	Tang dynasty begins (China)
668	Silla unifies Korea
710	Nara period begins (Japan)
794	Heian period begins (Japan)
918	Koryŏ conquers Silla (Korea)
938	Đại Việt ends Chinese rule in Việt Nam
960	Song dynasty begins, Neo-Confucianism spreads (China)

1009	Lý dynasty begins (Việt Nam)
1192	Rule of Kamakura shoguns begins (Japan)
1225	Trần dynasty begins (Việt Nam)
1271	Yuan (Mongol) dynasty begins (China)
1368	Ming dynasty begins (China)
1392	Chosŏn (Yi) dynasty begins, Neo-Confucianism spreads (Korea)
1428	Lê Dynasty begins, Neo-Confucianism spreads (Việt Nam)
1500s	Christianity introduced to East Asia
1603	Rule of Tokugawa shoguns begins, Neo-Confucianism spreads (Japan)
1644	Qing (Manchu) dynasty begins (China)
1802	Nguyễn dynasty begins (Việt Nam)
1868	Meiji period begins (Japan)
1887	French colonize Việt Nam
1910	Japan annexes Korea
1912	Qing dynasty ends
1930s	Japanese occupation of China begins
1945	Japan defeated, Korea and Việt Nam gain independence
1949	People's Republic of China established
1966	Cultural Revolution begins (China)
1975	Communists unify Việt Nam
1976	Death of Mao Zedong (China)
1990s–2000s	State support of Confucianism revived and continued (China)

Introduction

Confucius in East Asia

Visitors to Washington, DC, may be surprised to see Confucius there. He appears on the east pediment of the United States Supreme Court building, just to the left of the Athenian lawgiver Solon, who occupies the central position in a tableau of historical and symbolic figures, and just across from the Biblical prophet Moses, who stands on Solon's opposite side. Perhaps Confucius is depicted here because his ideas, alongside ideas from the West's Greek and Judeo-Christian heritages, inspired American "founding fathers" such as Benjamin Franklin, Thomas Jefferson, and James Madison. This relative ripple in the current of American culture originated with the tidal wave of influence that has washed over East

Figure I.1. Confucius (left) on south wall of the
United States Supreme Court. Photo by auther.

Asian cultures since at least 195 BCE, when the first emperor of China's Han dynasty first offered sacrifice at Confucius' tomb. It is difficult to overstate the enormous significance that this ancient Chinese thinker has had on the development of East Asia—the most economically robust, culturally diverse, and densely populated region on the planet, home to almost one out of every four human beings alive today. Simply put, it is impossible to understand this part of the world, its peoples, or its role in global history without knowing something about Confucius, Confucians, and Confucianism. This short book aims to provide such basic knowledge in the contexts of Chinese, Korean, Japanese, and Vietnamese history.

For East Asians, Confucius as an historical personality and spiritual symbol combines the significance and power associated with Socrates and Jesus. Indeed, along with Socrates, Jesus, and the Buddha, the twentieth-century philosopher Karl Jaspers called Confucius a "paradigmatic individual"—that is, a person who symbolically embodies the intellectual and spiritual culture to which he belongs even as he helps to define it.[1] Although this crucial figure wrote nothing at all, as far as modern scholars are concerned, he nonetheless became the author of mainstream East Asian cultures. For millennia, no East Asian regime has governed independently of Confucian influence, and since the seventeenth century, few serious moral, political, and social thinkers in the West have failed to consider Confucius' teachings. Even when Confucius and his tradition have been criticized or condemned, as has often been the case during the past century or so, they have been conspicuously present in East Asian affairs. One might argue that, without its history of state sponsorship, Confucianism as we now know it would not exist. Since each country in East Asia was governed by a Confucian-identified regime at the time of its first sustained contacts with the West, the history of Confucianism and the state is intertwined with the history of East-West exchange in China, Korea, Japan, and Việt Nam as well as the history of these countries' modern development.

Each of the following four chapters is devoted to a single country within the East Asian region as viewed through the lens of Confucianism's historical development, spiritual significance, social impact, and political role there. Every chapter is divided into four sections. First, the origins of Confucianism in that country are discussed. Because Confucianism is linked with the rise of classical East Asian civilizations, these sections also provide overviews of foundational historical events in each country. Next is an examination of how self-cultivation—the pursuit of intellectual, moral, and spiritual excellence as defined by the Confucian tradition—has been

Figure I.2. Altar at Confucian temple in Harbin, China. The banner above the altar reads (R-L) "The Way Spreads Great Harmony," a phrase that combines key terms from classical Confucian texts. Source: Wikimedia Commons, Prince Roy, http://commons.wikimedia.org/wiki/File:Harbin_Confucian_Temple.jpg.

practiced in its national context. The third section of each chapter deals with the historical impact of Confucianism on social ideas, institutions, and practices of the featured country. Since Confucianism first developed in China and spread from there to the rest of East Asia, the reader is advised to read chapter 1 before exploring the history of Confucianism in Korea, Japan, or Việt Nam, even if his or her primary interest in Confucianism lies outside of its Chinese context. In particular, the section of this chapter that is entitled "Confucianism and Chinese Society" may be especially

Map I.1. World map indicating extent of Confucian influence across the East Asian region, with China, North and South Korea, Japan, and Việt Nam depicted in shade. Source: Wikimedia Commons, Betoseha, http://commons.wikimedia. org/wiki/File:East_Asian_Cultural_Sphere.png.

valuable for those seeking to understand how the Chinese movement known as "Neo-Confucianism" influenced the development of Confucian cultures in Korea, Japan, and Việt Nam. Finally, each chapter considers the close ties that Confucianism has had with political institutions in each East Asian nation from antiquity to the present. Confucianism only became influential—first in China, and afterward across East Asia—after being adopted as a state ideology, and the relationship between Confucianism and the state continues to define the tradition in East Asia today.

This book concludes with a look at Confucianism in contemporary East Asia. In various ways, each of the nations profiled here has rehabilitated Confucius as a symbol with meaning for modern East Asians. The governments of China and Việt Nam, although nominally Communist in orientation, annually spend large amounts of money promoting Confucian festivals, paying for the renovation and upkeep of Confucian academies and temples, and generally borrowing the prestige associated with Confucius to enhance the international images of their respective countries. Although neither the modern Japanese nor the South Korean governments formally endorses Confucianism, the legacy of centuries of state support for Confucian traditions in these countries can be seen in everything from official school textbooks to the behavior of politicians in moments of national crisis. And government promotion of Confucianism (though sometimes contested) is hardly the full extent of the tradition's survival in modern times. Confucius and his tradition continue to serve as the basis for East Asian regional identity as well as a resource for individual Chinese, Koreans, Japanese, and Vietnamese seeking to make sense of contemporary life. The many different strands of this multifaceted modern Confucianism do not necessarily all tend in the same direction, but they do constitute a web of identity, meaning, and practice that still lies at the foundation of East Asian life.

Readers are encouraged to refer to the timeline of East Asian history that precedes this introduction as well as the glossary and "Suggestions for Further Reading" that may be found at the end of the volume. Note that the chronological designations "BCE" (Before the Common Era) and "CE" (Common Era), which correspond numerically to the traditional "BC" and "AD" designations, are used in both the timeline and the text. In most cases, terms in Chinese, Korean, Japanese, and Vietnamese are used only once in the text, with their English meanings substituted thereafter. All of the images found in this book are within the public domain and may be accessed online with ease using the source URLs that accompany each caption.

1

CONFUCIANISM IN CHINA

A time traveler from China's Qing dynasty (1644–1912 CE) who visited twenty-first-century China might be much less shocked by what he can see today than by anything that he might have observed after materializing at any point between the fall of the dynasty in 1912 and the death of the Communist leader Mao Zedong in 1976. In some ways, the role played by Confucianism in relation to the Chinese state in the first decades of this century is not so different from its role in China's imperial history. Unlike Mao, but very much like his predecessor Deng Xiaoping (1904–1997), Chinese President Xi Jinping has used Confucianism to lend intellectual, cultural, and moral credibility to a regime that otherwise might be seen as overly dependent upon imported models (both Marxist and capitalist) and consequently out of step with the deeply nationalistic ethos of today's China. This relationship between the regime and Confucianism requires that "Confucianism" provides at least some of its traditional content: commitments to moral integrity in service of society, the moral accountability of rulers to subjects, the goal of harmonizing social hierarchies, and the general valorization of Chinese cultural identity, which Xi has called "the cultural soil that nourishes the Chinese people." Xi has published his own commentaries on Confucianism, quoted Confucian classics in his public remarks, incorporated Confucianism into required study for Chinese Communist Party members and praised Confucianism as the key to "understanding the national characteristics of the Chinese as well as the historical roots of the spiritual world of the present-day Chinese."

But the engagement of China's contemporary government with Confucianism also has come at a cost to traditional Confucianism, which is due to its simultaneous commitment to Marxist values. This has had the effect of emptying Confucianism of much of its traditional content, at least in terms of its social force. Many have concluded that Xi's Confucianism is merely a way to shore up the Party's authoritarian rule by linking it to the volatile power of Chinese cultural nationalism, which then can be more easily controlled by the regime. After all, the regime selects its public servants by focusing on candidates' political ideology and loyalty to the Chinese Communist Party, rather than their personal virtue and knowledge of Confucian classics, as was (ideally) the case in centuries past. Yet students who hope to attain positions of power in contemporary China still are guided by principles found in Confucian texts

THE ORIGINS OF CONFUCIANISM IN CHINA

The Confucian *Analects* (Chinese *Lunyu*, a "collection of sayings" attributed to, or about, Confucius) begins in this way.

> Is it not pleasant to learn with a constant perseverance and application? Is it not delightful to have friends coming from distant quarters? Is he not a man of complete virtue, who feels no discomposure though men may take no note of him? (*Analects* 1:1)[1]

This saying has been memorized and recited by generations of East Asian students for millennia, and many Chinese, Korean, Japanese, and Vietnamese adults still can recall it in full, even if they no longer remember any other passages from Confucian texts. It encapsulates three core elements of what now is known as Confucianism: dedication to learning as a lifelong spiritual calling, emphasis on social relationships, and moral integrity despite the temptations of fame, power, and wealth. The man associated with these values was an obscure, itinerant Chinese teacher of aristocratic young men who lived in the late sixth and early fifth centuries BCE. Known in his lifetime as Kong Qiu ("Qiu of the Kong family"), but honored by later generations with the names Kongzi ("Master Kong") and Kong Fuzi ("Revered Master Kong," from which his Western name comes), Confucius has come to represent the ambitions, obligations, and aspirations of nearly every educated person in East Asia from antiquity to the present. In this sense, "Confucius" is less an historical individual and more a brand name or trademark for a particular combination of spiritual discipline, social ethics, and moral idealism unique to China and its neighbors.

Almost nothing about Confucius' early life is known apart from sources that were written not only long after his death, but also long after Confucianism was established as the primary intellectual, political, and religious force in elite Chinese culture. While these sources tend to present

8

Figure 1.1. The tomb of Confucius in Qufu, Shandong province, China. Source: Wikimedia Commons, Rolf Müller, http://upload.wikimedia. org/wikipedia/commons/0/07/Confuciustombqufu.jpg.

Confucius as a key participant in the major events of his time, all that is known for certain is that he was born in the small feudal state of Lu in what now is Shandong province in northeast China and worked as a teacher of traditional literature and ritual, occasionally serving as a low-level official in local government. He lived between the social instability of the "Spring and Autumn Period" and the descent into violence and chaos known as the

9

"Warring States Period." Many Chinese thinkers of this time looked back with nostalgia at the Western Zhou dynasty, which formerly ruled over a unified north central China between the eleventh and eighth centuries BCE. To such thinkers, including Confucius, it seemed that both society and the universe were out of alignment with the *Dao* or "Way" of natural and moral harmony. Confucius used Western Zhou culture to articulate his understanding of the Way and formulate a challenge to his own times.

The ruling class of the Western Zhou left behind a rich body of texts and traditions that Confucius and others mined for cultural, political, and spiritual resources. Western Zhou kings and officials performed elaborate rites of divination and sacrifice related to their ancestors, spent enormous amounts on costly grave goods and monuments, combined political and religious authority in the person of the king, and relied upon a bureaucratic organization to sustain court life and society's needs. Their historical documents, governmental decrees, poetry, and ritual texts later were given the title "classics" or "scriptures" (*jing*) by Confucius and his followers. For Confucians, the most important elements of Western Zhou tradition had to do with the deity Heaven (*Tian*) and its relationship to human history and morality.

According to Western Zhou texts, the dynasty rose to power by overthrowing its predecessor, the Shang dynasty, in 1045 BCE. Having established themselves as the new rulers of the north central Chinese plain, its elites developed a religious ideology to explain their place in history and justify their authority. According to Western Zhou thought, the Shang god Shang Di ("The Lord on High") once affirmed the Shang kings' high moral stature by allowing them to rule. By proving itself unworthy of this mandate, however, the Shang lost its heavenly legitimacy and was forced to surrender to the virtuous founders of the Western Zhou. Moreover, the Western Zhou equated Shang Di with Heaven and thus claimed that Heaven had revoked its support of the Shang and placed the Western Zhou in power.

Many scholars think that the concept of Heaven in Western Zhou culture developed out of the worship of Western Zhou royal ancestors. The practices of offering sacrifice to one's ancestors and consulting them about the meaning and direction of one's affairs probably is the oldest aspect of Chinese religious culture. Ancient Chinese veneration of Heaven, ancestor worship, and divination practices shared a common purpose: to maintain harmonious relations between this world and the next for the benefit of the human community. *Analects* 1:11 records several sayings of Confucius on the importance of reverence for one's ancestors: "Observe what a person has in mind to do when his father is alive, and then observe what he does when his father is dead. If, for three years, he makes no changes to his father's ways, he can be said to be a good son." Similarly, Confucius credited Heaven as the source of his moral merit (*Analects* 7:23). Confucius studied and taught Western Zhou texts such as the *Shijing* (*Classic of Poetry*) and the *Yijing* (*Classic of Changes*) because he believed that they reinforced these basic views and values.

Other Western Zhou texts, such as the *Shujing* (*Classic of Documents*), tell the story of the dynasty's rise and fall. The early years of the dynasty were plagued by civil war. At the heart of this conflict was the matter of royal succession. The brother and chief minister of the dynastic founder, the Duke of Zhou, argued that Heaven had bestowed its mandate on all of the Western Zhou people, especially the king's ministers, rather than on the royal lineage alone. Other factions at court, however, countered that the king alone was the recipient of divine authority. Unsurprisingly, this argument prevailed with Zhou kings. Yet the Duke of Zhou's view that Heaven's mandate is gained and maintained by merit rather than blood eventually became very influential on Confucius and his followers much later. Confucians would come to see the Western Zhou's collapse in 771 BCE as an act of Heaven that signaled the dynasty's loss of the heavenly mandate to rule. The story of the Western Zhou's beginnings, however, convinced Confucians that, just as virtuous rulers once came to power and brought prosperity and harmony, so too could sage kings walk the earth again in their own time and order society with tradition, ritual, and virtue.

Confucius and his disciples came from the social class known as *shi* ("retainers" or "knights"), who traditionally served the Western Zhou kings. With the collapse of the Western Zhou order, these men became lordless anachronisms and fell into genteel poverty and itinerancy. Their knowledge of ancient aristocratic traditions, however, helped some of them reinvent themselves as advisers to the competing, rulers of the "Warring States," who hoped to reunify the former Western Zhou territory by patterning their court rituals and other institutions after those of the fallen dynasty. Confucius himself is said to have held such a position, albeit only for a short time before withdrawing into retirement as a ritual master and teacher of future court advisers. His students and their followers later shaped Confucius' teachings and view of the Chinese past into what became Confucianism.

Map 1.1. Map of Warring States China. Source: Wikimedia Commons, https://commons.wikimedia.org/wiki/File:EN-WarringStatesAll260BCE.jpg.

CONFUCIANISM AND CHINESE SELF-CULTIVATION

In a life thoughtfully lived according to Confucian teachings, the three core elements of Confucianism outlined in *Analects* 1:1—dedication to learning as a lifelong spiritual calling, emphasis on social relationships, and moral integrity despite the temptations of fame, power, and wealth—are supported and developed by a set of practices and guiding values that go back to Confucius' earliest interpreters. Like Buddhism or Christianity, in some ways Confucianism as a tradition was shaped most powerfully not by its founder, but by those who succeeded him as influential teachers within his lineage of authority. Two of the most influential early Confucian thinkers after Confucius' time were Mengzi ("Master Meng," c. 372–289 BCE), better known in the West as Mencius, and Xunzi ("Master Xun," c. 310–220 BCE). These two thinkers shared a commitment to Confucius' teachings, but differed radically in their interpretation of those teachings.

Both Mencius and Xunzi based their interpretations of Confucian thought and practice around theories of human nature, even though, according to the *Analects*, Confucius had very little to say about this subject.

Mencius taught that "by fully developing one's mind, one knows one's nature, and by knowing one's nature, one knows Heaven." (*Mencius* 7A1) For Mencius, the human journey toward morality begins with birth as a being that naturally is oriented toward goodness, much as a seedling naturally is oriented toward sunlight and future development as a full-grown plant. (In classical Chinese, the words for "humanity" and "goodness" sound very similar and are written with characters that share common graphic elements.) One then proceeds toward maturity, guided by the examples of ancient sages and the ritual forms and literature they have left behind. This helps to explain the consistent emphasis on rote memorization of texts and practices found throughout Confucian traditions, both in China and elsewhere. Habitually doing what is morally right, one eventually uplifts oneself from the merely human to sagehood, as Heaven intends.

Although the graphic elements of Chinese characters do not always reflect their etymologies, the components of the character for "sage" tell a revealing story: the person who can master or rule over what is heard as well as what is said can be called "sage" (or "saint"—in classical Chinese, this character suggests the meanings of both English words). Nature is crucial to moral development, but so is nurture. Mencius' model of moral psychology involves both discovery (that human nature is good) and development (through which human nature can be made even better). His ideas can be found not only in the text that bears his name, but also in other early Confucian writings such as the *Zhongyong* (*The Doctrine of the Mean*) and the *Daxue* (*The Great Learning*).

耳	+	口	+	王	=	聖
er (ear)		*kou* (mouth)		*wang* (ruler)		*sheng* (sage, saint)

Although Mencius' theory of human nature became the basis for most Confucians' understanding of self-cultivation, Xunzi's theory also found favor among some Confucians prior to the Han dynasty. Xunzi was born in the state of Zhao during the late fourth century BCE, which means that he is unlikely to have met Mencius and certainly never knew Confucius. Like Mencius, Xunzi apparently was employed by the state of Qi and also held office in the state of Chu. He and his disciples questioned many of Mencius' teachings, especially his claim that human beings are born with a predis-

Figure 1.2. Painting by Su Hanchen (twelfth century, China). Source: Wikimedia Commons, http://commons.wikimedia.org/wiki/File:Su_Hanchen,_Playing_Children.jpg.

position toward goodness. Some of his disciples, such as Li Si and Han Fei, later abandoned the Confucian tradition altogether and even served the anti-Confucian Qin dynasty that eventually unified the "Warring States," an event that Xunzi may have lived to see as a very old man.

For Xunzi, human beings are born with a natural tendency toward selfishness and disorderly conduct, which can be overcome only through the corrective power of culture. Both Mencius and Confucius pinned their hopes for society's renewal on the appearance of a sage-ruler who would combine political power with moral wisdom, unify the fractured empire, and usher in a new age of harmony and prosperity. According to Confucius, "One who rules by morality may be compared to the North Star—it occupies its place and all the stars pay homage to it." (*Analects* 2:1) While

Mencius taught that rulers who failed to exercise their power in accordance with Heaven's mandate invited rebellion and replacement, Xunzi envisioned the ruler-subject relationship in familial terms, with the ruler as the all-powerful father entrusted with the care of his dependent subjects, who in turn benefited from his wise choices in matters of education policy and other cultural affairs.

Despite their differences, both Xunzi and Mencius believed that human beings are capable of moral self-transformation. Both argued that cultural development through ritual and textual education was the key to achieving this self-transformation. The idea that human beings are incapable of moral self-transformation is completely alien to the Confucian tradition. In this sense, Confucian thought has no concept analogous to the Christian notion of "original sin." This apparent optimism about human beings probably is the most significant view shared by Confucianism's founders, and most likely played a role in helping ideologies with similar views of human improvability, such as Buddhism and Marxism, to spread during later periods of Chinese history. Although they approach it by different means, these three traditions share the goal of enabling the flower of innate human goodness to grow.

CONFUCIANISM AND CHINESE SOCIETY

Confucianism is an intrinsically social phenomenon. Classical Confucian texts, such as the *Analects*, are the result of a social process of intergenerational consensus and transmission of ideas, institutions, and practices, even when the text in question largely is the work of an individual thinker, such as Mencius or Xunzi. The Confucian classic known as the *Xiaojing* (*Classic of Filial Piety*) exemplifies this quality by presenting Confucian teachings through a dialogue between Confucius and his disciple, Zengzi, about filial piety (respect for one's elders). The very first chapter states:

> Once upon a time, when [Confucius] was unoccupied, and [Zengzi] was sitting by in attendance on him, the Master said, "The ancient kings had a perfect virtue and all-embracing rule of conduct, through which they were in accord with all under heaven. By the practice of it the people were brought to live in peace and harmony, and there was no ill-will between superiors and inferiors.... [This virtue of] filial piety is the root of all virtue, and the stem out of which grows all teachings.... It commences with the service of parents; it proceeds to the service of the ruler; it is completed by the establishment of oneself."

Although the unifying Qin dynasty was hostile to Confucians, by the end of the succeeding Han dynasty in the third century CE, Confucianism had become the mainstream ideology of Chinese society and remained influential even as Chinese began to embrace new traditions such as Buddhism and the Daoist sects that appeared in response to Buddhism's arrival in China. Tales of moral exemplars, intended to promote Confucian values, were circulated among families and in private academies attended by the sons of the elite. Young people were taught to emulate paragons of filial piety such as Wu Meng, who compensated for his parents' lack of mosquito netting by secretly encouraging hordes of the insects to bite him while his parents slept peacefully through the night.

> [His parents] were so touched that their sounds of sobbing could be heard by the neighbors. From all sides the neighbors gathered to investigate the matter, and learned about Wu Meng's sacrifice on behalf of his parents. Everyone thought that the boy's attitude of filial respect was most remarkable, especially for one only eight years old. Someone reported the incident to the local magistrate, who wrote a memorandum to the Dragon Throne, to inform the imperial court. The matter thus came to the attention of the Emperor, who rewarded Wu Meng with a scholarship to the [state-sponsored Confucian] academy [which trained students for official careers]. Further, he gave the family a set of mosquito nets and a stipend, so that they never again lacked the necessities of life.[2]

Confucian models for self-cultivation such as Wu Meng competed in China's spiritual marketplace with rival models advocated by Buddhist texts such as the *Xuepenjing* (*Blood Bowl Scripture*). The *Blood Bowl Scripture* tells the story of Mulian, a monk who makes a horrific journey to the Buddhist hell realms in order to save his rather unpleasant mother, who has been reborn there in accordance with her atrocious karmic demerits. However, popular Buddhist morality tales such as this one show how powerful Confucian teachings about filial piety were in Chinese society. Even foreign religions had to incorporate such Confucian elements in order to be attractive to Chinese people. The inscribed stone monument erected in the Chinese capital by Christian missionaries from West Asia during the Tang dynasty (618–907 CE), does not mention Jesus Christ's crucifixion or resurrection (both of which might have seemed alien to Confucians). However, it does use Confucian language to describe the "filial and just" Tang emperors who allowed Christianity to be introduced to China, saying that their "principles embraced those of preceding monarchs" and praising their "cultivation of truth and rectitude."[3]

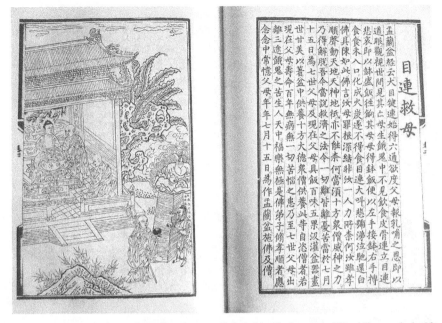

Figure 1.3. Depiction of Mulian interceding with Shakyamuni Buddha on behalf of his mother (lower right corner of illustration), who has been reborn as a hungry ghost. Source: Wikimedia Commons, http://upload.wikimedia.org/wikipedia/commons/e/e7/Moggallana_saves_his_mother.jpg.

The influence between Confucian and Buddhist traditions also flowed in the opposite direction, especially during the centuries after the Tang dynasty, when Buddhism became a permanent element in China's religious landscape. By the Song dynasty, practices such as meditation and concerns such as metaphysics played a much greater role in Confucian self-cultivation than ever before. Confucian scholars who saw themselves as restoring the meaning of ancient texts often reinterpreted these writings from perspectives shaped as much by Buddhist mysticism and monastic discipline as traditional Confucian concerns for social harmony and personal rectitude. The great twelfth-century "Neo-Confucian" revivalist, Zhu Xi, presented early works such as the *Analects* and the *Great Learning* as ways of penetrating profound mysteries, discerning cosmic patterns or principle, and tracing the pathways of vital energies or material force in the universe. His manual of household morality and ceremony became standard reading for all educated families, while pious Confucians everywhere followed his instructions for divination using the Classic of Changes by preparing and purifying themselves morally through meditation. This infusion of Buddhism was intensified under the influence of the sixteenth-century general, official, and teacher Wang Yangming, who broke with Zhu Xi's outwardly-focused tradition and taught his disciples to "get rid of selfish human desires and preserve the principle of nature, which is like refining gold," much as Chan (Zen) Buddhist masters instructed their students to seek the inner Buddha-nature. Having absorbed Buddhist (and Daoist) elements, Confucianism became more influential on Chinese society than ever before.

By the beginning of the Ming dynasty in the late fourteenth century, being Chinese was inseparable from being Confucian, even though Chinese cultural norms encouraged followers of one tradition to participate in the institutions and practices of others. Confucianism now was first among its peers in the social and spiritual landscape of China. At the same time, what distinguished Confucians from others in traditional China still distinguishes them today: ultimately, Confucian self-cultivation is inspired by China's past, carried out in a social matrix, and serves the family, the community, and the state as well as the individual.

CONFUCIANISM AND THE CHINESE STATE

Despite the obscurity in which Confucius and his early followers lived and labored, for most of the past two thousand years Confucianism has been synonymous with the state in China. Beginning in 136 BCE, Confucian texts became the basis of the imperial government's civil service examinations, making Confucian thought a mandatory subject for those who wished to obtain official employment. From this time through the nineteenth century, most candidates for government office in China were required to pass examinations based on their knowledge not only of the "Five Classics" of Western Zhou literature, but of the standard Confucian interpretations of these texts. Throughout the empire, state-sponsored temples to Confucius served as academies for would-be officials and centers of worship according to Confucian rites.

Participation in Confucian ceremonies and mastery of Confucian teachings brought family pride, community fame, and government approval and employment. At the age of eighteen, a young man called Bai Juyi passed the imperial civil service examination, thus paving the way for his eventual success as a high government official and leading member of China's literati during the ninth century. He wrote a poem to commemorate his achievement, which begins with these words:

> For ten years I never left my books;
> I went up . . . and won unmerited praise.

Figure 1.4. Candidates for the civil service examination await their results (Qiu Ying, sixteenth century). Source: Wikimedia Commons, http://upload. wikimedia.org/wikipedia/commons/f/f9/Civilserviceexam1.jpg.

> *My high place I do not much prize;*
> *The joy of my parents will first make me proud.*[4]

In keeping with Confucian tradition, service to the state was understood to be a mode of self-cultivation. Faithful and upright performance of one's civic duties not only fulfilled one's social obligations, but also brought one into harmonious relationship with the universe. Regardless of whether the reigning emperor personally favored Buddhism, Daoism, or no particular religious tradition, all Chinese emperors functioned as sacred symbols of Confucian authority and, as "Sons of Heaven" (the traditional Chinese imperial title), provided a direct link between Heaven and humanity. As the architect of what some have called "imperial Confucianism," the Han dynasty thinker and official Dong Zhongshu put it this way: "As for the one who appropriates the mean of Heaven, Earth, and humankind and takes this as the thread that joins and connects them, if it is not one who acts as a king, then who can be equal to this task?"[5] For almost two millennia, Confucianism was sustained by the textual canon, educational institutions, and spiritual ethos developed by Dong and elaborated upon by his successors. Without Confucius, there would be no Confucianism; but

19

without the support of the Chinese state, there would be no Confucianism as it has been known for the past two thousand years.

Just as Chinese emperors came to be seen as divine representatives of the Confucian Way on earth, the figure of Confucius himself was transformed by his tradition's relationship with the state. Han dynasty chroniclers such as Sima Qian included fantastic elements in their biographies of Confucius. In such tales, Confucius' birth was heralded by a *qilin* (a unicorn-like creature) and dancing dragons, he was born with the texts of the Western Zhou classics inscribed on his body, and he grew to be nine feet tall. After his death, he was alleged to have revealed himself in a glorified state to his living disciples, who then received further esoteric teachings from their by then-deified master. With the state's blessing, Confucius was the recipient of worship in official Confucian temples. The twentieth-century Chinese philosopher Feng Youlan once suggested that, had these images of Confucius prevailed, Confucius would have become a figure comparable to Jesus Christ in the history of China, and there would have been no arguments among scholars about whether or not Confucianism was a religion like Christianity.

With renewed government backing during the Song and Ming dynasties, Confucianism expanded beyond China into Korea, Japan, and Việt Nam, where these new forms of the tradition exercised powerful and lasting influence.[6] But as Confucian ideas, institutions, and practices came to dominate East Asian culture, politics, and society, a number of Confucian thinkers became critical of the tradition. Advocates of the "Han [Chinese] Learning" and "Evidential Learning" movements accused Confucian thought of being overly abstract or mystical and called for a return to the allegedly more worldly and practical Confucianism of the Han dynasty. By the late Qing dynasty, leading Confucians increasingly emphasized the concrete, objective, and practical value of Confucianism for rulers as well as ordinary people. This emphasis led to the Confucian sponsorship of what might be called empirical research, some of which was inspired by exposure to Western methods, although it usually was confined to historical topics or policy issues rather than the natural sciences.

Even as nineteenth-century Confucians tried to reform their tradition, the state that they served was proving itself unable to meet the challenges of both Western imperialism and a rapidly modernizing Japan. After suffering humiliating defeats by both Western powers (after the anti-foreign Boxer Uprising of 1900) and Japan (in the first Sino-Japanese War of 1894–95), the Confucian civil service examination system was dismantled. This late concession to modernity was not enough to save the dynasty, however, and the last Qing emperor was deposed in 1912. To many thoughtful people in China and elsewhere, Confucianism now seemed synonymous with imperial China's impotence, obsolescence, and failure.

Between the fall of the Qing dynasty in 1912 and the victory of the Communist revolution in 1949, the Chinese political world was divided between those who condemned "the shop of Confucius' family" as an obstacle to modernization and those who sought to redeem the Confucian tradition for the twentieth century. Sun Yat-sen, the "Father of the Nation" and architect of the post-imperial Chinese state, which embraced Western ideologies such as democracy and socialism, praised Confucianism.

> We must revive not only our old morality but also our old learning. If we want to regain our national spirit, we must reawaken the learning as well as the moral ideals which we once possessed. What is this ancient learning? Among the human theories of the state, China's political philosophy holds a high place. . . . China has a specimen of political philosophy so systematic and so clear that nothing has been discovered or spoken by foreign statesmen to equal it. It is found in the [early Confucian classic] *Great Learning.*[7]

Like Sun, the Kuomintang (Chinese Nationalist Party) leader Chiang Kai-shek employed Confucian rhetoric, while the Chinese Communist Party leader Mao Zedong bitterly condemned the tradition as a tool of feudal oppression.

After the triumph of Mao's forces and the establishment of the Communist People's Republic of China in 1949, mainland China became an inhospitable zone for Confucian thinkers. Intellectuals such as Liang Shuming, who combined Confucian thought with elements of Buddhism, Marxism, and Western liberal democracy and argued that traditional Chinese thought (i.e., Confucianism) was superior to Western thought, suffered public criticism and humiliation at best and imprisonment and execution at worst, especially during the "Cultural Revolution" of the late 1960s and early 1970s. Many Confucian scholars fled to Taiwan, Hong Kong (then a British colonial possession), and the West. As university professors and public intellectuals, these thinkers reestablished Confucianism primarily as an academic endeavor, but also as a resource for anti-Communist ideology. Outside of the People's Republic of China, Confucianism came to be seen as an engine of economic progress and source of cultural strength for ethnic Chinese and other East Asians.

Figure 1.5. Depiction of "Red Guards" (revolutionary youth) in a Chinese primary school textbook, 1971. Source: Wikimedia Commons, Villa Giulia, http://upload.wikimedia.org/wikipedia/commons/c/c1/Red_Guards.jpg.

To almost everyone's surprise, the relationship between Confucianism and the Chinese state reversed itself once again in the late twentieth century after decades of harsh anti-Confucian rhetoric by the Chinese Communist Party and other critics. Beginning in the 1980s, the mainland Chinese government began to "rehabilitate" the image of Confucius, sponsoring academic conferences and publications devoted to Confucianism, establishing "Confucius Institutes" to encourage appreciation of Chinese culture all over the world, and even awarding a "Confucius Peace Prize" to "promote world peace from an Eastern perspective." Confucius and Confucianism have become the subjects of best-selling books, popular television shows for children and adults, required high school and university courses, and multi-million dollar movies. For a few strange months during the first half of 2011, a 31-foot bronze statue of Confucius even stood in Beijing's Tiananmen Square, just a short distance from Mao's tomb. The statue later disappeared as mysteriously as it appeared, without any explanation from the Chinese government.

Figure 1.6. A young girl wearing *hanfu* (traditional Chinese clothing) as part of her coming-of-age ceremony in 2013. Source: Wikimedia Commons, hanfulove, https://upload.wikimedia.org/wikipedia/commons/6/64/Jili3.jpg.

Many attribute the sudden revival of Chinese state interest in Confucianism to the spiritual vacuum left by the perceived failure of Mao's ideology in contemporary China, a country that by many economic measures now is second only to the United States, and that by other metrics already has surpassed it. While scholars and diplomats disagree as to whether China truly has become Confucian once again, it is clear that Confucianism plays a role in China's reemergence as a regional and global power—both because its government endorses Confucian ideology and because many of its people see Confucianism as a source of contemporary Chinese identity. As China's middle class—the world's largest—looks for ways to signal both its wealth and its virtue, frequently its members turn to Confucian pageantry, such as renting or purchasing expensive traditional clothing (*hanfu*) for staging their children's coming-of-age ceremonies in purpose-built, well-lit ritual venues, where they can be documented lavishly on cellphone video. Less ostentatiously, the elevation of Dr. Li Wenliang (1985–2020, the opthalmologist in the city of Wuhan who first warned Chinese authorities about the spread of COVID-19 despite pressure to keep it quiet) to nationwide heroic status after his death from the disease echoes many aspects of traditional Confucian hagiography. Strikingly, it was the head of the school of Chinese classics at Wuhan's Central China

Normal University, who publicly took the Chinese government to task for ignoring Li's warnings and contributing to his premature death and called upon other scholars to emulate Li's moral example by reflecting on themselves and speaking up for the welfare of the Chinese people. In doing so, he invoked the traditional Confucian expectations that governments should benefit their subjects while their educated subjects, in particular, must use their voices to make sure that governments do so. "We all should reflect on ourselves," he wrote, "and the [Chinese government] officials should rue their mistakes even more."[8]

2

CONFUCIANISM IN KOREA

In 1954, the Geneva Conference famously failed to resolve the political division of the Korean peninsula between its Communist north and Capitalist south. A tenuous ceasefire between the opposing halves of the country began, symbolized by a 250-kilometer-long demilitarized zone (DMZ) that separates the two. At a comfortable distance of some 200 kilometers from the DMZ is the South Korean city of Andong, a traditional center of Confucian learning and the hometown of the sixteenth-century CE Confucian thinker Yi T'oegye. Near a resort built in the style of a *hanok* (traditional Korean house) is a combination theme park and museum complex known as *Yugyo-landeu* ("Confucian-Land"). Visitors to "Confucian-Land" are treated to a presentation on the challenges and atrocities of modern life, such as consumerism, hypersexualization of youth, and violence, before being ushered through a "time tunnel" into the deeply Confucian Korea of Yi T'oegye, where everyone is described as having lived in perfect harmony despite the rampant social and gender divisions of the time, thanks to their adherence to Confucian teachings, "the root of Korean spiritual culture."[1] It can be baffling for those who associate South Korea with well-choreographed boy bands, professional video gaming, and luxury cosmetics, rather than Confucian scholars and premodern virtues, but that seems to be the point of the place.

Not far from Andong is the city of Kimje, where the young scholar Kim Su-yeon founded a Confucian academy in 1954. Interviewed in 2011, the 86-year-old Kim said:

> There is a road that men walk, and there is another road that animals walk. But these days the difference between them is not clear. Learning these [Confucian] texts would help people go right on the road that men walk.[2]

Kim's reply says a great deal not only about what Confucianism means to older Koreans today, but also about what Confucianism has meant to

Figure 2.1. Chehwajeong Pavilion in Andong, South Korea, built in the early nineteenth century by the Confucian scholar Yi Hano to house his elderly mother. Source: Wikimedia Commons, 문화재청 (Cultural Heritage Administration), https://upload.wikimedia.org/wikipedia/commons/5/53/안동_체화정.jpg

Koreans throughout its history in the peninsula. For most Koreans over the past two thousand years or so, Confucianism has been identified largely with writings about a human-centered moral order best promoted through educational institutions. Since its introduction to Korea sometime during the first few centuries CE, Confucianism has been associated with textual traditions imported from China but adapted to the social and spiritual needs of the Korean people. Indeed, Koreans have prided themselves on being Confucius' true inheritors, especially at times when the Confucian heritage in China seemed to be in jeopardy, and historically Korea has functioned as the major transmitter of Confucian and other Chinese traditions to Japan. Finally, Confucianism's power to shape Korean culture has been most acute at moments of crisis and division among Korean peoples.

THE ORIGINS OF CONFUCIANISM IN KOREA

Confucianism's history in Korea begins with China's relationship to the peninsula during the Han dynasty, which established four "commanderies" or garrisoned colonial outposts in what now is North Korea during the second century BCE. Foremost among these was the commandery of Lelang, which endured until 313 CE in the area of the modern North

Figure 2.2. Exemplars of filial piety painted on lacquered basket recovered from Lelang, c. 25-220 CE. Source: Wikimedia Commons, http://commons. wikimedia.org/wiki/File:Painted_figures_on_a_lacquer_basket,_Eastern_Han_Dynasty2.jpg.

Korean capital city of Pyongyang. Among the artifacts recovered from the Lelang site is a lacquerware "painted basket" found in an official's tomb, on which are depicted ninety-four scenes of people carrying out filial actions, which attests to the presence of Confucian values in that area.[3] Apart from artifacts such as this, however, little is known of Confucianism's early interactions with Korean culture.

Ironically, given Confucianism's often contentious history in relationship to Buddhism, it was through Buddhism that Confucianism first reached a Korean audience. Like China, Korea encountered Buddhism at a moment of political division in its long history. At the time of the earliest known Korean Confucian institutions, the "Three Kingdoms" of Koguryŏ in the north, Silla in the southeast, and Paekche in the southwest competed for supremacy until the defeats of Paekche and Koguryŏ by Silla in the 660s.

Buddhism became attractive to would-be unifiers of the peninsula as a cosmopolitan tradition that linked local courts to an international network of artistic, economic, literary, philosophical, and political exchange sustained by Buddhism's expansion across the Asian continent through the Silk Road as well as Korean-dominated maritime routes. Even as Buddhism was adopted as the official doctrine of various Korean states, Buddhist monks and institutions were the primary transmitters of Confucian traditions to Korea (and through Korea to Japan).

Map 2.1. The "Three Kingdoms" of the Korean peninsula near the end of the fifth century CE. Kaya, a small fourth state later annexed by Silla, also appears on this map. Source: Wikimedia Commons, Chris 73, http://upload.wikimedia.org/wikipedia/commons/7/77/Three_ Kingdoms_of_Korea_Map.png.

The synthesis of Buddhist and Confucian teachings known as the *Hwarangdo* (Way of the Flower Boys) formed the basis of an elite organization for young men that existed in Silla from its unification of the southern peninsula in the 660s until the fall of the regime in the tenth century. Its activities included the study of Confucian morality as well as Buddhist arts, and members were indoctrinated to observe "five commandments for secular life," the first three of which conspicuously reflect Confucian values:

1. Loyalty to one's lord
2. Filial piety toward one's parents and teachers
3. Trust in one's friends
4. No surrender in battle
5. No taking of life without just cause

This combination of Buddhism and Confucianism helped to cement southern Korea's political and social unification during the last few centuries of the first millennium CE and led to the adoption of Confucianism as the basis for a Chinese-style civil service examination system in both Unified Silla (668–935) and its successor state of Koryŏ (918–1392), from the name of which the modern term Korea is derived.

By the tenth century, Koryŏ scholars such as the Chinese-educated ex-Tang dynasty official Ch'oe Ch'i-wŏn (857–924?) characterized Korean religion as a blend of Buddhist, Confucian, and Daoist traditions, and legends about the sanctity of Ch'oe and other well-known Korean Confucians took on elements of each of these religions. For example, in the eleventh century, the Koryŏ ruler King Hyŏnjong posthumously granted Ch'oe an honorary Confucian title, and by the 1200s, his image was enshrined as an icon to be worshiped in what became the National Confucian Academy. Ch'oe also was deified as a Daoist immortal and regarded as a pious Buddhist whose inscriptions provide much of the information about Buddhism in Unified Silla that is available today. These developments suggest that Confucianism was not perceived as radically distinct from other imported religious traditions, especially Buddhism, during the eras of Unified Silla and Koryŏ (918–1392). Confucianism was seen as an important but subordinate teaching within a larger spiritual universe dominated by Buddhism.

Nonetheless, the power of Confucianism as an intellectual, spiritual, and social force in the Korean peninsula was growing, especially as Buddhism lost institutional support and international prestige in the wake of its persecution by China's Tang emperor Wuzong in 845. Koryŏ statesman Ch'oe Ch'ung established a Confucian curriculum divided into nine courses based on the *Zhongyong* (*Doctrine of the Mean*), and other classical Chinese texts. In the later tenth century, influenced by Confucian advisers, Koryŏ's King Kwangjong simultaneously emancipated slaves and established a civil service that was open to all males except serfs and the bastard sons of Buddhist monks. Efforts such as these eventually built up sufficient momentum to spur Koryŏ's King Injong's suppression of a

Buddhist-led rebellion against his regime in 1135. He also sponsored the compilation of a Confucian-style chronicle of the pre-Koryŏ history of the peninsula (the earliest such text), the *Samguk Sagi* (*History of the Three Kingdoms*), and founded six Confucian colleges in his capital city, each reserved for the sons of particular ranks within the hierarchy of the Koryŏ elite. Young men from families associated with the two lowest rungs of Koryŏ officialdom also could apply to study at the local Confucian academies that began to appear at this time. By the eleventh century, private Confucian schools also had begun to operate throughout Koryŏ. The six colleges in the Koryŏ capital eventually were amalgamated into a National Confucian Academy at which virtually every Korean Confucian matriculated until the early twentieth century.

Together, institutions such as these reinforced connections between Korean elites and Chinese culture; for example, Yuan dynasty (1271–1368) records indicate that many graduates of advanced Korean Confucian educational institutions went on to distinguish themselves in China's competitive civil service examination system. These institutions also reinforced the view of Confucianism as a gateway to government service and political power in Koryŏ and paved the way for Confucianism's gradual replacement of Buddhism as the dominant ideology of Korean society. By 1363, all candidates for the Koryŏ civil service examination were required to study at the National Confucian Academy. Finally, by linking Confucian education to a stratified set of career pathways, they also reinforced a kind of caste system that divided members of Korean society into four hierarchically-ranked categories: (1) gentry, including Confucian scholars, (2) farmers, (3) artisans, and (4) merchants—a system that eventually came to dominate Japanese society, as well. All of these developments set the stage for the dawn of Confucianism's golden age in Korea.

CONFUCIANISM AND KOREAN SELF-CULTIVATION

The story of Confucianism's development into the preeminent path for personal self-cultivation in Korea begins with the inauspicious example of a fourteenth-century Confucian martyr murdered by his king, Chŏng Mongju.

Better known by his pen name, P'o Ŭn ("Secret Garden"), Chŏng Mongju was a distinguished Koryŏ official who also taught at the National Confucian Academy and represented Koryŏ as a diplomat in China and Japan. But the Koryŏ that Chŏng served had been reduced to a vassal

Figure 2.3. Late-nineteenth-century portrait of Chŏng
Mongju. Source: Wikimedia Commons,
http://upload.wikimedia.org/wikipedia/commons/9/96/
Goryeo-Portrait_of_Jeong_Mongju-02.jpg.

regime of Yuan (Mongol) China. When the Yuan regime collapsed in
1368, Koryŏ elites were divided between those who remained loyal to their
Mongol allies and those who supported China's fledgling Ming dynasty.
Twenty years later, Yi Sŏngkye, a Koryŏ general tasked with expelling
Ming forces from territory north of the Yalu River, famously decided to
turn back at the border between Koryŏ and China and rebel against his
sovereign. Marching his army southward, General Yi captured the Koryŏ
capital, executed the Koryŏ king, and took the throne for himself, thus
establishing the Yi or Chosŏn dynasty. Chŏng was among those who
criticized the actions of General Yi (now King T'aejo) as treacherous and
immoral.

King T'aejo's son and heir, King T'aejong, invited Chŏng to a banquet in the new capital of Kaesŏng, perhaps as a ploy to strengthen the new regime's legitimacy by associating it with a respected sage. At the banquet, however, Chŏng reiterated his unwavering loyalty to Koryŏ. On his way home, Chŏng was intercepted by five minions of King T'aejong who beat him to death on the Sŏnjuk Bridge. In death as in life, Chŏng was seen as a paragon of the Confucian virtue of loyalty, as exemplified by the following poem attributed to him:

> Even if I may die, die a hundred times,
> Even if my skeleton may become dust and dirt,
> And whether my spirit may be there or not,
> My single-hearted loyalty to my lord will not change.

This poem cemented Chŏng's reputation as a Confucian martyr. His disciples adopted the second syllable of his pen name (Ŭn) as a suffix for their own, retired as a group from government service, and founded private academies in various rural areas. The Sŏnjuk Bridge became a popular pilgrimage site and eventually was closed to traffic. Ironically, King T'aejong's heirs honored Chŏng's principled opposition to their ancestors by granting his image a place in the National Confucian Academy's worship hall. In the meantime, Chŏng's disciples helped spread Confucianism beyond official circles, which led to a new era for Confucianism as the basis for personal self-cultivation as well as institutional education in Korea.

The Confucianization of Korean spirituality would have to wait until the work of another fourteenth-century Confucian Chŏng, Chŏng Tojŏn, was complete. This Chŏng was descended from commoners who had risen to official status through four generations of education and effort. Unlike the martyred Chŏng Mongju, Chŏng Tojŏn embraced the Chosŏn regime, seeing service to the usurper as a means of putting Confucian principles into practice. He became the most trusted adviser of King T'aejo, who eventually endowed him with top civil, diplomatic, and military authority in Korea, subject only to the Chosŏn throne. Thus empowered, Chŏng Tojŏn moved quickly to establish Confucianism as the supreme ideology of the Chosŏn state, arguing that it was superior to its rivals Buddhism and Daoism insofar as "managing the world," "saving the people," and "ruling the nation" were concerned. The network of educational institutions, government offices, religious polemics, and social hierarchies that Chŏng Tojŏn set into motion toppled Buddhism from its previous position as the primary shaper of Korean spiritual life and established Confucianism in its place. For his pains, he was rewarded with brutal assassination by Yi Pangwŏn, who as the Chŏson king was notorious for his ruthless tactics. Despite (or perhaps because of) this second Confucian martyrdom at the hands of the Chŏson regime, the Chŏson period would be remembered as the grand era of Confucianism as the foundation of the Korean individual, society, and state.

The Confucianism promulgated by Chŏng Tojŏn and like-minded Korean literati was the Confucianism taught by Song dynasty Chinese masters such as Zhu Xi, who integrated Buddhist and Daoist meditation and metaphysics into his understanding of classical Confucian texts and traditions and promoted this ethical and cosmological synthesis as the basis for all of society.[4] Key to this so-called "Neo-Confucianism" are two related concepts: vital energy or material force, and cosmic pattern or principle. For Chŏson Confucians such as Yi Yulgok, the cosmic pattern or basic framework of the universe was essentially unified, but its manifestations or expressions in the form of vital energies were multiple, just as the moon in the nighttime sky is one but reflections of moonlight on various earthly surfaces (e.g., ponds, windows, mirrors) are many. Equipped with this understanding of the universe's underlying moral framework, Koreans schooled in Chŏson Confucianism could see their individual dispositions and actions as expressions and fulfillments of cosmic purpose. In a letter written to his friend Sŏng Hon (1535–1598), Yi Yulgok uses the metaphor of water in a vessel to explain Confucian understandings of human nature and its relationship to cosmic structure:

> When the vessel moves, the water moves—which is like material force issuing and principle mounting it. The vessel and the water move together; there is no difference between the vessel's moving and the water's moving. Nor is there a difference in the issuance of material force and principle. . . . When the vessel moves, the water necessarily moves; the water never moves of itself. Principle is nonactive; it is material force that has activity.[5]

According to Yi Yulgok's metaphor, the cosmic pattern or "Dao Mind" embedded within all things also can be found within one's own vital energy or "Human Mind." His use of Buddhist- and Daoist-sounding language is not coincidental, as he spent time as a Zen Buddhist monk and dabbled in Daoist practices prior to his conversion to Confucianism at the age of twenty. This innate cosmic pattern cannot be manifested apart from human activity; like water in a vessel that is picked up, the two move together inseparably. Developing oneself through study of Confucian classics, practice of Confucian ritual arts, and obedience to Confucian morality is how the cosmic pattern unfolds. This vision of personal self-cultivation as a powerful mode of participation in, and fulfillment of, the grand plan and purpose of the cosmos was intensely appealing to many Chŏson Confucians.

However, once Chŏson Confucians began applying themselves to the project of manifesting cosmic pattern in their personal spiritual development, they also began to argue amongst themselves about the relationship between the personal and the cosmic. This argument, famously known as the "Four-Seven Debate," concerned how to interpret passages from two different classical Confucian texts, the *Mencius* and the *Liji* (*Record of Ritual*). According to *Mencius* 2A6, human nature originally is good, and evidence of this can be found in four "sprouts" or types of innately good human emotional responses: compassion, shame, modesty or deference to others, and feelings of approval or disapproval. Yet the *Record of Ritual* enumerates not four, but seven different innate emotional responses:

1. Joy
2. Anger
3. Sorrow
4. Fear
5. Love
6. Dislike
7. Desire

These "feelings" encompass what might be called "negative" or "bad" as well as "positive" or "good" dispositions of the human mind, all inborn and unlearned. If everything, especially the individual human mind and the broader cosmic order, was interconnected in original and pure goodness, then how could the apparent discrepancy between the *Mencius* and the *Record of Ritual* be accounted for? Since Chŏson Confucians not only constructed their individual spiritual journeys, but also the entire worldview of educated Koreans, around the unity of "Dao Mind" and "Human Mind," a great deal stood to be gained or lost in the resolution of this debate about how the two related to each other.

Against Yi Yulgok's contention that "Human Mind" and "Dao Mind" were one, the aforementioned Yi T'oegye maintained that the four "sprouts" or "beginnings" were expressions of cosmic pattern (ideal or spiritual),

Figure 2.4. South Korean thousand-*won* banknote depicting the Confucian academy (Tosan sŏwŏn) established in memory of Yi T'oegye in 1574. Source: Wikimedia Commons, Steve46814, http://upload.wikimedia.org/wikipedia/commons/9/9a/Korea-Andong-Dosan_Seowon_3016-06.JPG.

while the seven "feelings" were merely expressions of vital energy (real or material). Like a horse and its rider, Yi T'oegye said, cosmic pattern rides on vital energy in order to express itself in the world. Without vital energy, cosmic pattern could not appear; but without cosmic pattern, vital energy would be directionless and chaotic.

In the end, this debate confirmed Chŏson Confucians' fundamental preference for the teachings of Zhu Xi and other Song dynasty Confucians, which emphasized the larger collectivities of society and the cosmos as paths toward individual self-cultivation—and not the other way around, as Buddhism, Daoism, and alternative forms of Confucianism (such as the teachings of Wang Yangming, whose work was condemned as unorthodox by Chŏson Confucians), tended to suggest. Ultimately, the debate's sharpening of distinctions central to Confucian self-cultivation led to the monopoly of Confucianism over the determination of Korean social values.

CONFUCIANISM AND KOREAN SOCIETY

Chŏson Confucianism embodies a paradox found in many great cultural traditions. On the one hand, the teaching and activism of Chŏson thinkers such as Yi T'oegye and Yi Yulgok suggested an ideal of moral

Figure 2.5. Eighteenth-century Korean ink painting of a dragon.
Source: Wikimedia Commons, Honolulu Academy of Arts,
http://upload.wikimedia.org/wikipedia/commons/6/6a/Korean_
ink_and_color_painting_of_dragon%2C_18th_century%2C_
Chos%C3%B4n_dynasty%2C_Honolulu_Academy_of_Arts.jpg.

egalitarianism, according to which all subjects of the Chŏson king theoretically were capable of pursuing self-cultivation to the point of becoming Confucian sages. On the other hand, the actual society in which Chŏson subjects lived was deeply stratified, with very limited opportunity to climb out of hereditary social classes and categories, which themselves were legitimated by Confucian institutions and values.

One example of this paradox can be seen in Chŏson Confucians' use of classical texts such as the *Classic of Changes*. Yi T'oegye addressed the Chŏson king on the topic of the first hexagram listed in the text, "*yang*" or "generativity" (☰), the commentary of which mentions "an arrogant dragon [that] will have cause to repent." According to Yi T'oegye, this meant that a ruler who does not seek the advice of scholars and other officials dedicated to Confucian learning will lead his state into disaster. He urged the king to avoid this fate by relying on Confucian ministers when making important decisions that could improve or worsen ordinary Koreans' lives.

At the same time, Chŏson Confucians enshrined the *yangban* class (the highest two social orders, consisting firstly of civil officials and secondly of military officials) at the pinnacle of both social and spiritual development. Members of these families enjoyed preference over those from artisanal, agricultural, and low-status backgrounds and quickly came to dominate the civil service examination system that led to official appointments and social supremacy. Similarly, men were elevated above women, and the aged above the young, in terms of their capacity for self-cultivation and social authority. A Chŏson woman was taught to remain faithful to her husband, even and especially following her husband's death, after which she was not supposed to remarry for fear of appearing unfaithful or sexually promiscuous. At the same time, a Chŏson man of sufficient financial means and social standing was permitted to maintain relationships with women other than his wife—usually women who came from lower-class backgrounds and who were regarded as "concubines" rather than "wives," which usually meant that sons born to such unions had no legal right to their father's estate and were prohibited from taking the civil service examinations or pursuing high government office. To their credit, some Chŏson Confucians protested against such inequalities and prejudices, but for the most part, Confucian institutions in Chŏson Korea were complicit in the oppression of the poor, the young, and the female. The reforming ambitions of early Chŏson Confucians such as Chŏng Tojŏn gradually were replaced by the self-interested maintenance of the social order by those at its top.

One reaction to the connection between social suffering and Chŏson Confucianism was the reform movement known as *Sirhak* ("Practical Learning"), which arose during the eighteenth century. *Sirhak* thinkers such as Sŏngho Yi Ik, a failed civil service examination candidate, accused orthodox Korean Confucianism of neglecting social welfare:

The sages wrote [the *Classic of Changes*] to discuss the fundamental way to govern the nation. It reads: "The great virtue of heaven and earth is life. The big treasure of the sages is position. The key to keep the position is benevolence. The method to attract people is financial administration. Righteousness means managing finances properly, having the right language, and forbidding the people from making mistakes."[6]

Yi Ik and other *Sirhak* reformers—most of whom held no official position—pressured the orthodox Chŏson Confucian establishment to lighten the burden of social hierarchies, rethink the civil service examination system, limit the authority of the king, redistribute land to empower disenfranchised peasants, and become more open to science and other forms of "Western" learning then being introduced to East Asia. To some extent, they promoted Korean nationalism at a time when Korean Confucianism was deeply China-centered, even though many Chŏson Confucians were critical of their Qing dynasty counterparts. Some *Sirhak* thinkers attempted to prove that ideas introduced through Western science actually could be found in Confucian classics.

As Koreans increasingly became aware of Western science, political philosophies, and religious traditions, it became more important for Chŏson Confucians to mount an effective defense against these foreign rivals. As early as 1601, Koreans were introduced to Roman Catholicism through the distribution of texts originally aimed at converting Ming dynasty China. The same struggles and conflicts that defined Catholicism's initial experience in China occurred as some Koreans converted to the new faith. Catholic clergy, imagery, and theology struck many Chŏson Confucians as reminiscent of Buddhism, so it was an easy matter for them to recycle centuries-old anti-Buddhist polemics for use against Catholicism. Like Buddhism before it, Christianity was handicapped by its apparent challenge to Confucian filial piety. A Korean convert calling himself Paul Yun was executed publicly in 1791 for burning his family's ancestor tablets, an important element in the Confucian family rituals mandated by Chŏson law and custom, but which Yun and other converts saw as pagan idols. Christian talk of a coming messiah who would restore justice and liberate the downtrodden sounded suspiciously like the many Buddhist movements that had championed rebellion in the name of the future Buddha, Maitreya, and alarmed conservative Confucian political sensibilities. European scientific knowledge and technology introduced by Christians also disturbed Confucian worldviews rooted in classical Chinese texts. Above all, the Christian doctrines of one, absolute, transcendent God and humanity's original sin seemed most threatening to Chŏson Confucianism. As a result, a strongly nationalistic form of Confucianism known as *Tonghak* ("Eastern Learning") developed in order to counter Western influence in general, and Christian influence in particular, in Korea.

Against Christian theism and the doctrine of original sin, nineteenth-century *Tonghak* thinkers such as Choi Sihyong argued that the Confucian "Way" of Heaven was identical with the universal moral mind of all human beings, so that there was no need to appeal to a transcendent source of morality or salvation as Christians do. Choi and other anti-Christian voices in Korea depicted Confucianism as a tradition that equated moral goodness with truth, human nature, and social harmony and Christianity as a tradition that associated moral goodness with its God's revelation in the Bible, the atonement of Christ, and individual salvation. From this perspective, Christianity (like Buddhism before it) was an alien, otherworldly faith that promoted selfish individualism while Confucianism was a familiar, practical tradition that promoted social stability. In 1866, the Chŏson government followed the lead of *Tonghak* ideology by authorizing the mass slaughter of French Catholic missionaries and their Korean congregations.

Other nineteenth-century *Tonghak* leaders went even further in their campaign against Christianity. Son Pyŏng-hŭi founded a highly political new religious movement based on Confucianism, Ch'ŏndogyo ("Teaching of Heaven's Way"), which rejected the idea of afterlife, opposed feudal social structures, and advocated a utopian social order in the name of Confucian tradition. This expression of *Tonghak* ideology found favor with many impoverished Korean peasants, who also were attracted to the setting of its teachings to easily-memorized tunes. Most late Chŏson Confucianism remained mired in medieval debates, and it became apparent that the destiny of Confucianism in Korea was linked to the destiny of the Chŏson state, which seemed doomed to collapse under pressure from Western and Japanese colonialism alike.

CONFUCIANISM AND THE KOREAN STATE

Chŏson Korea was the first East Asian state to adopt "Neo-Confucianism" as its exclusive official ideology and the last to "open" itself to Western influence. The Chŏson regime's relationship with Confucianism was key to both its rise to power and its eventual fall in the early twentieth century.

Figure 2.6. Portrait of Son Pyŏng-hŭi (1861–1919).
Source: Wikimedia Commons, https://commons.
wikimedia.org/wiki/File:SonByeongHui.jpg.

As Qing dynasty China tottered and newly-modernized Meiji period Japan asserted itself to both its East Asian neighbors and its Western rivals, Koreans increasingly questioned the relevance of the Confucian-identified state. In an effort to restore its legitimacy and vitality, the Chŏson King Kojong promoted social reforms and retitled himself the "Emperor" of Korea in 1897, but ten years later, he was compelled to abdicate and confined to his palace by Japanese forces, which had occupied Korea as a "protectorate" since 1905 and formally annexed the country as a colonial territory in 1910. Almost a decade later, the ex-"Emperor" died under house arrest in his palace under suspicious circumstances.

Confucianism became the target of criticism by Korean nationalists who saw it as too foreign (that is, Chinese—despite Korea's millennia of independent Confucian tradition), too antiquated (that is, anti-scientific

Figure 2.7. Photograph of a Confucian scholar in late Chŏson Korea, taken sometime before 1910. Source: Wikimedia Commons, http://upload.wikimedia.org/ wikipedia/commons/d/de/Korean_Confucian_scholar.JPG.

—despite Korean Confucians' interest in science), and too oppressive (that is, monarchical, feudal, and sexist—despite Korean Confucians' challenges of royal absolutism and advocacy of social reforms) to be of any use to a nation in crisis. The reputation of Confucianism in Korea was not enhanced by Japan's reliance on Confucian ideas, institutions, and practices to bolster its colonial rule. It is telling that, once Korea was liberated from Japanese rule in 1945, the most compelling visions for Korea's future were not Confucian, but rather Western, i.e., liberal-democratic and Marxist, in origin.

The political division of the newly independent Korean peninsula in 1945 into an American-controlled southern zone and a Soviet-controlled northern zone was intended by the Allied powers to be a temporary transition to unification, but by 1948, parties on both sides of the 38th parallel (the line of latitude marking the north-south border in the peninsula) claimed to represent the true government of the country. By 1950, Communist troops from the north had invaded the south, and war raged for the next three years, exacerbated by the involvement of both Chinese and American military forces. From 1953 until the present, only an armistice agreement—not a full peace treaty recognizing the end of hostilities—has prevented further outbreaks of violence between the northern Democratic Republic of Korea and the southern Republic of Korea.

Confucianism has fared very differently in North and South Korea since the Cold War division of the peninsula. In South Korea, fear of Communism propelled one brutal autocrat after another into executive office until 1987, when demands for democratic processes, civil rights, and economic reforms won out. All six governments that have presided over South Korea since 1948 have endorsed Confucian rituals, sites, and values to some extent, partly in order to remind Koreans north and south of the threat to traditional culture posed by communism. At the same time, South Korean leaders have not hesitated to criticize Confucianism when they have seen it as opposed to modern goals such as economic development. School textbooks produced by the South Korean state echo this official ambivalence about Confucianism: they emphasize Confucian moral exemplars of loyalty, service to society, and zeal for learning, but they also describe Confucianism as an ideology that disappeared with the fall of the Chŏson state in 1910. The position of Confucianism in South Korea is complicated by the remarkable growth of Christianity since the early twentieth century. While South Korean followers of Confucian new religious movements such as Ch'ŏndogyo are counted in the hundreds of thousands at most, the estimated number of Christians in South Korea (both Protestant and Roman Catholic) amounts to approximately thirty percent of the population. More than half of South Korea's presidents, including several who were notoriously corrupt as well as others who were famously principled social justice activists, have identified as Christians. However, perhaps as many as one-fourth of Korean Protestants have distanced themselves from formal church membership due to concerns that South Korea's evangelical megachurches, in particular, ignore social justice in favor of focusing on personal salvation, which might be called a Confucian reason for dropping out of church. Despite the unpleasant history of Confucian-Catholic relations in premodern Korea, in contemporary Korea many Roman Catholics embrace aspects of Confucian tradition, especially *jesa* (ancestor veneration), which was sanctioned by Pope Pius XII in 1939. Both Confucian-minded Korean traditionalists and many Korean Christians find themselves discomfited by contemporary South Korea's changing views of gender and sexuality. In general, it seems that Korean Catholics are more attuned to Confucian values than many of Korea's most visible Protestant institutions, but Confucian principles such as family-centeredness and respect for social hierarchy survive in both of Korea's Christian communities, albeit in Christianized forms.[7]

Due to North Korea's secretive government, it is difficult to say a great deal about the fate of Confucianism there. Officially, religious activity – including participation in Confucian movements such as Ch'ŏndogyo, which according to the government claims the allegiance of more than ten percent of its citizens—is tolerated by the North Korean state, but in practice it seems that religious institutions are permitted to exist only as long as they do not challenge the Communist regime. However, if one looks beyond obvious labels such as "Confucian," a great many legacies of Confucian tradition can be seen in the highly ritualized public ceremonies, Kim family political dynasty, devout anti-capitalism, and cult of deceased leaders that distinguish the North Korean state.

Figure 2.8. The South Korean national flag. Source: Wikimedia Commons, http://commons.wikimedia.org/wiki/File:Flag_of_South_Korea.svg.

Perhaps the most powerful symbol of Confucianism's enduring alliance with the Korean state is the national flag of South Korea, designed during the late Chŏson period under the auspices of King Kojong and used as the Chŏson state flag from 1883 to 1910. Each of its visual elements is based on Confucian symbology, especially as found in the *Classic of Changes*: the central icon of *T'aegŭk* (the Great Ultimate, illustrating the dynamic binary complementarity of *yin* and *yang*), the four trigrams (representing, from upper left clockwise to lower left, heaven, water, earth, and fire), and the surrounding white background (symbolizing the original moral purity of human beings). Moreover, each of the trigrams depicted on the flag correlates with a specific Confucian virtue, family role, and cosmic element.

TRIGRAM	VIRTUE	ROLE	ELEMENT
HEAVEN ☰	goodness	father	wood
WATER ☵	wisdom	daughter	water
EARTH ☷	modesty	mother	fire
FIRE ☲	righteousness	son	metal

Today, South Korea is among the most modern countries in the world, and ancient ideologies such as Confucianism might seem to be out of place there. Yet various expressions of Confucian identity, from the crass and commercial ("Confucian-Land") to the quiet and principled (Kim Su-yeon's academy), survive. The future of the Korean peninsula is uncertain, but it seems likely that if unification ever does occur, Confucianism will play some part in knitting together the divided Korean people.

3

CONFUCIANISM IN JAPAN

THE ORIGINS OF CONFUCIANISM IN JAPAN

The early 2020s were an interesting time for anyone curious about Confucianism's legacy in contemporary Japan. On the one hand, in September 2020, Japan's Keio University announced the discovery of a 1,400-year-old manuscript copy of the *Lunyu yishu* (pronounced as *Rongo giso* in Japanese), a set of commentaries on Confucian classics written by the Chinese scholar Huang Kan (502–557 CE) but lost in China since the 1100s CE. Believed to have been brought to Japan by Japanese diplomats around the time of its completion between the late sixth and early seventh centuries, this copy remained in the possession of the powerful Fujiwara clan for several centuries before passing into the hands of the imperial court sometime during the Edo period (1603–1868 CE) before disappearing. This discovery was regarded as so monumental that it inspired a special public display of the ancient scrolls at the Maruzen Bookstore's main branch (Tokyo's largest) that October.[1] For some, this seemed to confirm the lasting importance of Confucianism even in hyper-modern twenty-first-century Japan. Even now, it appeared, Confucian values were considered as central to Japanese cultural identity, more than a millennium after they first were introduced to the archipelago.

On the other hand, it was not quite six months later that Japan's Supreme Court ruled that the municipal government of Naha in Okinawa prefecture had violated post-1945 Japan's constitutional principle of separation between politics and religion by allowing a Confucian temple, the *Shisei-byō* ("Temple of the Perfect Sage"), to operate rent-free on public land in the city.[2] Naha lies on the East China Sea coast in Japan's southernmost prefecture, which was part of the independent Ryūkyū Kingdom (1429–1879 CE) until its annexation by Japan after centuries of domination. Historically, the Okinawan islands cultivated close ties to China and attracted many highly skilled and well-educated Chinese immigrants, some of whom became ancestors of the Kingdom's officials.[3] The Confucian temple that stands there today was built in 1975 to replace its predecessor, which dated back to the 1600s but was destroyed in the Battle of Okinawa (March 26–July 2, 1945). Like the older temple, the newer structure has functioned as a venue for Confucian education, meetings of the local *Sōseikai* ("Society of the Ancestral Sages," i.e., Confucian Association), and the performance of Confucian rituals, such as an annual ceremony to welcome back the spirit of Confucius to the premises. It was these ritual performances in particular that decided the case as far as the Supreme Court justices were concerned, since they "considered [the ritual] a religious activity" and therefore "judged [the temple's exemption from rent] as giving a helping hand to a particular religion." The verdict was the result of seven years of litigation instigated by a woman activist. One might conclude that, for contemporary Japanese, Confucianism is an unwelcome reminder of Japan's historical dependency on Chinese culture in an era of prickly Sino-Japanese relations, as well as an obsolete symbol of patriarchal values in a feminist age.

It would be a mistake to draw simplistic conclusions based on either of these recent episodes in Confucianism's long history in Japan. While

Figure 3.1. The Shiseibyō or Confucian temple in Naha, Okinawa, Japan. Source: Wikimedia Commons, 663highland, https://upload.wikimedia.org/wikipedia/commons/7/7f/Naha_Siseibyo03n2700.jpg.

it is true that Confucianism still influences many basic Japanese cultural practices and social values, it is not necessarily true that contemporary Japanese people are as devoted to this Chinese tradition as their ancestors, who eagerly imported hand-copied Confucian manuscripts at great expense and risk to themselves. Nor is it necessarily the case that judicial verdicts, no matter how earthshattering, reflect a wholesale shift in the customs and attitudes of the Japanese population. (Consider the widespread opposition to the legalization of same-sex marriage in Japan despite the March 2021 finding of a Sapporo court that the lack of this legal option is unconstitutional, not to mention the decision of some Japanese cities to issue non-legally-binding "certificates of marriage" to same-sex couples.[4]) Both of these incidents echo aspects of Confucianism's origins in Japan, which are deeply intertwined with China's projection of cultural and political power as well as Japan's selective embrace of technologies and traditions from continental East Asia as a means of civilizational advancement.

THE ORIGINS OF CONFUCIANISM IN JAPAN

Japan's introduction to Confucianism may have occurred as early as 108 BCE, when Han dynasty Chinese diplomats stationed in "commanderies" (garrisoned colonial outposts established in what now is north Korea) began to make voyages of exploration in the strait between the Korean peninsula and the Japanese islands. By the third century CE, various Japanese communities had experienced multiple contacts with both Korean and Chinese societies. Chinese historical writings describe what now is Japan as a series of mountainous islands southeast of Korea inhabited by almost thirty separate communities of "eastern barbarians," each with its own ruler and tributary relationship to Chinese courts, but collectively known to the Chinese as *Wo*, the land of "dwarves" (pronounced *Wa* in Japanese). They also mention a woman called Pimiko, who ruled over a territory in Wa known to the Chinese as Yamatai and whom the governor of the Daifang commandery in north central Korea regarded as a tribute-paying vassal of China. Early Chinese reports depict the Japanese as a short-statured, politically divided, and relatively uncivilized people who are ignorant of Confucian gender hierarchies and prone to Daoist superstition, although they praise Pimiko for her loyalty and filial piety as expressed in subordinate relation to China.

Rulers such as Pimiko may have seen alliances with Korean and Chinese regimes as a way to gain an advantage over their rivals for control of the archipelago, both in terms of political clout and technological

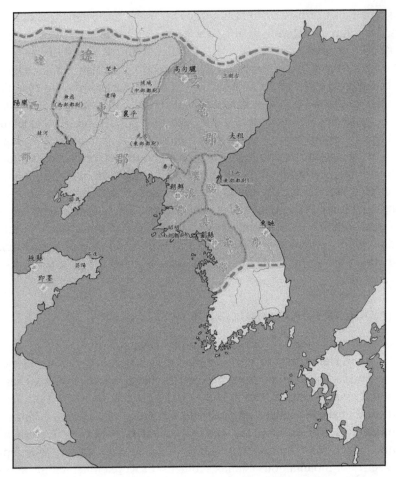

Map. 3.1. Map of Chinese commanderies on the Korean peninsula, with Japan's southernmost islands indicated at bottom right. Source: Wikimedia Commons, Evawen, http://upload.wikimedia.org/wikipedia/commons/5/52/Four_Commanderies_of_Han.jpg.

development. Certainly, early Japanese archeological sites from the Yayoi era and the subsequent Kofun or "ancient tomb" period reveal an abundance of Chinese- and Korean-made goods, including bronze mirrors and vessels, jade, swords, and other items associated with royal power in mainland East Asia during classical times. Since the Japanese lacked a writing system for their spoken language which is completely distinct from Chinese, classical Chinese script offered Yamatai elites the opportunity to become literate and participate in the textual world of cosmopolitan East Asia. By the 400s, at least some Japanese were able to read and write classical Chinese, and as a result, all early Japanese texts were written in

Figure 3.2. Depiction of Prince Shōtoku on a ten-thousand-*yen* note issued by the Bank of Japan in 1958. Source: Wikimedia Commons, Bank of Japan, http://upload.wikimedia.org/wikipedia/commons/8/85/P94b-10000Yen-%281958%29_front.jpg.

classical Chinese and thus reflect strong Confucian influence. Although Confucianism's fortunes were on the wane at this time, due to the collapse of the Confucian-identified Han dynasty and the subsequent rise of Buddhism and Daoism to prominence, Confucian learning remained the basis of East Asian regimes, and the Buddhist institutions sponsored by many Chinese and Korean courts helped to transmit Confucian texts and traditions to Japan as a form of overseas development aid. The flow of Confucian influence increased as refugees from conquered Korean states settled in Japan during the sixth and seventh centuries. By 600, the Japanese tradition of independent female rulership was fading away, young Japanese men were being sent at government expense to study Buddhism and Confucianism in China, and the *de facto* ruler of early-seventh-century Japan, regent Prince Shōtoku felt confident enough to address Emperor Yang of China's Sui dynasty as a peer and to question China's use of the term "dwarf" to describe his people, replacing it with the Chinese character meaning "harmony."

The figure of Prince Shōtoku looms large in any account of early Japanese history. Although he often is identified as a champion of Buddhism and became the recipient of fervent Buddhist devotion after his death, the documents associated with him suggest that Confucianism was just as important to his unifying regime. Within a decade of his appointment as regent by his aunt, Empress Suikō, Shōtoku had established diplomatic relations with China, implemented the Confucian court rank hierarchy already in use in Sui dynasty China and the Korean states of Koguryŏ and Paekche, and converted the Japanese calendar to the Chinese system based on the Five Processes (a cosmic cycle of interactions between the five elements of wood, fire, earth, metal, and water). The "Seventeen-Article Constitution" promulgated by Shōtoku respectfully acknowledges Buddhism at many points, but begins and ends with Confucian sentiments:

> Harmony is to be valued, and contentiousness avoided. . . . When those above are harmonious and those below are conciliatory and there is concord in the discussion of all matters, the disposition of affairs comes about naturally. Then what is there that cannot be accomplished? . . . [T]he leading principle in governing the people consists in ritual decorum. . . . To turn away from that which is private, and to set our faces towards that which is public—this is the path of a minister. . . . Matters should not be decided by one person alone.[5]

This document technically remained in force until the promulgation of the Meiji emperor's Constitution in 1890. Its language embodies Shōtoku's embrace of both Confucian and Buddhist traditions, a synthesis that set into motion the transformation of Japan from an isolated and disunified island chain into a centralized imperial regime deeply connected to East Asian cultural, political, and religious networks.

That process further unfolded during the reign of his later successor, Emperor Kōtoku, who ascended to the throne through a *coup d'état* and used his newfound power to proclaim what became known as the *Taika* reforms. These reforms began with the confiscation of private land by the state but eventually had a far-reaching impact, leading to the implementation of a Confucian legal system known as *Ritsuryō*, the establishment of a Chinese-style capital city, and the imposition of a two-tiered social hierarchy, each with its own subdivisions, similar to Confucian caste systems found in Tang dynasty China and the Korean state of Koryŏ. The upper class included four distinct ranks of persons associated with the imperial palace and other official appointments, while the lower class included imperial staff, guards at imperial tombs, various sub-officials, servants of the elites, and at the bottom, the slaves belonging to members of the imperial court and the leading clans. Perhaps most significantly, these reforms led to the acquisition of a new title by Japanese rulers. Formerly known as *Ōkimi* ("Great King," the traditional title of Japanese monarchs since Pimiko) and for a time during the early 600s called *Tenshi* ("Son of Heaven," a direct transliteration of the traditional Confucian title used by Chinese emperors), Japanese rulers now were called *Tennō* ("Heavenly Sovereign," a term borrowed from Chinese that connoted both Confucian and Daoist ideas of absolute imperial authority). By 710, the *Tennō* ruled from a palace in the capital city of Nara, the plan of which was based on the Tang dynasty capital of Chang'an. Thus empowered, the emperors of Japan moved to complete the work, begun by Shōtoku and his ancestors, of establishing a Chinese-style Confucian state that could rival China itself.

One of the foremost instruments of this effort was the compilation of official histories, written in Confucian style using classical Chinese, by scribes at the Nara court. The *Kojiki* (*Record of Ancient Matters*), completed in 712, purported to narrate the genealogy of Japanese emperors from the seventh century BCE through the third century CE, thus making the Japanese imperial line appear far older and more enduring than China's Tang dynasty, which ascended to the throne less than a century before the *Kojiki*'s compilation. A companion text, the *Nihon Shoki* or *Nihongi* (*Chronicles of Japan*) was completed in 720 and described the creation of the world, beginning with the Japanese archipelago, by deities (*kami*) who turned out to be the ancestors of the Japanese imperial family, as well as subsequent historical events through the early 700s. Both texts frequently use Confucian as well as Daoist rhetoric and terminology to describe what allegedly are events and figures that date back far before Japanese contact with these traditions:

> ... [T]hough the primeval beginnings be distant and dim, yet by the ancient teachings do we know the time when the lands were conceived and the islands born; though the origins be vague and indistinct, yet by relying on the sages of antiquity do we perceive the age when the deities were born and men were made to stand. ...[6]

> Our imperial ancestors and imperial parent, like gods, like sages, accumulated happiness and amassed glory.... From the date when Our Heavenly ancestor descended until now it is over 1,792,470 years.... When Heaven establishes a prince, it is for the sake of the people. The prince must therefore make the people the foundation. For this reason the wise sovereigns of antiquity, if a single one of their subjects was cold and starving, cast the responsibility on themselves.[7]

Despite the efforts of the imperial court to present Japan as an equal or even rival of Tang dynasty China, the Confucian discourse so familiar to Japanese elites during the Nara period had little impact on the lives of ordinary people in Japan at that time. To most Japanese commoners and

Figure 3.3. Depiction of *sankyō* ("Three Teachings" of
Confucianism, Buddhism, and Daoism), personified by Confucius
(left), Shakyamuni Buddha (center), and Laozi (right). Source:
Wikimedia Commons, ZEN 8, http://upload.wikimedia.org/
wikipedia/commons/8/8e/Three.Doctrines.jpg.

probably not a few elites, Confucianism appeared inseparable from Daoism
and Buddhism (each of which received far more imperial patronage), and
all three were integrated with the worship of traditional Japanese deities
in court-sponsored rituals as early as 701. Well into the Heian period,

during which Buddhism absorbed both Daoism as well as the worship of *kami* and attained its greatest success as a religion of the Japanese elite, Confucianism was described by influential thinkers such as Kūkai (Kōbō Daishi) as an important but subordinate tradition in relation to Daoism and especially Buddhism:

> Treatment differs with each physician. Human duties were preached by Confucius; on learning them one becomes a high government official. [The Daoist sage] Laozi taught the creation by yin and yang; on receiving his instructions one can observe the world from the tower of a Daoist temple. Most significant and profound is the teaching of the ultimate path of Mahāyāna [Buddhism]..... [T]he Three Teachings.... can be compared to the sun [Buddhism], the moon [Daoism], and the stars [Confucianism]."[8]

Buddhism remained a key element of both successful political regimes and popular religious movements as the stable imperial polity of the Heian period gave way to the shaky rule of *shōguns* (military dictators) during the Kamakura period. As late as the sixteenth century, Confucianism's influence in Japan was marginal in comparison to that of Buddhism, even though Confucianism had become the dominant ideology in both Chinese and Korean societies by that time. What had not yet happened in war-torn Japan, but already had occurred in Song and Ming dynasty China and Chŏson Korea, was the fusion of Confucian ideology with an authoritarian social order controlled by a powerful ruler.

CONFUCIANISM AND JAPANESE SELF-CULTIVATION

Despite its origins in turbulent Warring States period China, Confucianism has tended to prosper most during periods of relative social stability. In East Asian cultural history, Confucian influence typically has not become widespread until the problems of national identity, political disunity, and religious competition have been solved in a particular culture. In Japan, Confucianism had to wait a long time before conditions were satisfactory for its full-blown emergence as a popular spirituality as well as a state ideology. After seizing power in 1192, the *shōguns* struggled to impose order on the chaos that was post-Heian Japanese society. The chronic civil war that raged throughout the next four centuries and the two attempted invasions by the allied Yuan (Mongol) dynasty China and Korean state of Koryŏ in 1274 and 1281 were not the only challenges to achieving social stability. Devastating earthquakes, fires, floods, famines, epidemics, tsunamis, and typhoons, striking at regular intervals, also weakened Japanese physical and cultural infrastructure. Although new forms of Buddhism such as Zen rapidly became popular, the involvement of some Buddhist institutions in military affairs sullied their reputation among commoners and aristocrats alike. The introduction of Roman Catholic Christianity through Jesuit missionaries in the mid-sixteenth century complicated the Japanese social landscape even further. Despite the challenges to Christian conversion encountered in Japan, the Jesuits eventually claimed more than 100,000 Japanese converts, including several *daimyō* (feudal lords) and their *samurai* (retainers). Fearing the threat of European invasion under the guise of missionary activity, the warlords who were in the process of unifying Japan imposed various restrictions and persecutions on Christianity until the religion was outlawed completely in 1614 by Tokugawa Ieyasu, the first of a new, much more powerful, and much longer-lasting dynasty of *shoguns*.

Legal codes issued during the Tokugawa or Edo period make clear the general alignment of the shōgun's policy goals with the ideal social order envisioned by Confucianism. A document written by one samurai in 1619 and addressed to commoners instructs them to:

> [[c]onsider the Lord of your domain, the sun and the moon.... Treat your village head as if he were your own father.... Take heed that this advice is adhered to.... [If it is not] you may lose the support of the way of heaven, come to the end of the rope, be scorned by your lowly peer groups, and regret the incident forever. Always remember that such a misfortune can befall you.[9]

Samurai, the only class permitted to bear arms, were expected to distinguish themselves in Confucian learning and set a positive example for the rest of Tokugawa Japan's highly stratified society. As a result, educated Japanese and other molders of public opinion began to rediscover the spiritual treasures of Confucianism that their ancestors had overlooked in favor of Buddhism or the worship of *kami*. They happened to do so at a time after which "Neo-Confucian" movements in China and Korea already had revitalized the tradition and established it as a popular ideology.[10] Although Japan never instituted a Confucian-based civil service examination system like those found in China, Korea, and Việt Nam, other institutional conduits of Confucianism existed in Japan, such as the hereditary class of Confucian instructors at the imperial court academy. Zen monasteries maintained close links with China and promoted Confucianism as an adjunct to Buddhism through educational outreach programs in *terakoya* or "temple schools." These soon were joined by local Confucian academies that began to spring up all over Japan. Gradually, nearly all members of Tokugawa society began to look to Confucianism as their primary guide for living.

In keeping with Chinese and Korean intellectual and spiritual trends, the first form of "Neo-Confucianism" embraced by Japanese thinkers was the tradition of the Song dynasty sage Zhu Xi. Its initial Japanese advocates, such as the seventeenth-century intellectual Fujiwara Seika, taught that Confucianism offered the answer to Japan's chronic social instability because of its "clarification of human relationships." Having learned about Confucianism during his tenure as a monk at the prestigious Shōkokuji Zen Buddhist temple in Kyōto as well as from Korean prisoners of war, Fujiwara became a committed if non-doctrinaire Confucian and eventually was appointed to teach Tokugawa Ieyasu himself. Commenting on Zhu Xi's favorite Confucian classic, the *Great Learning*, he writes:

> The character 大 ["Great"] signifies both the unity of self and other, and the unity of inner and outer. 'Unity of self and other' refers to 'manifesting luminous virtue' and 'having affection for the people'; in other words, making no distinction between self and other.... [W]hen you no longer distinguish between self and other, or between inner and outer, you will know the meaning of 大. The character 学 ["Learning"] should not be interpreted exclusively as book learning.[11]

Like Zhu Xi, Fujiwara Seika saw personal self-cultivation through the perfection of one's social relationships as the goal of Confucian practice. Yet, unlike its Chinese and Korean counterparts, Fujiwara's brand of "Neo-Confucianism" did not take sides in the doctrinal conflict between the lineages of Zhu Xi and his Ming dynasty critic, Wang Yangming. Instead, Fujiwara blended elements of both traditions, as well as Buddhism and Daoism, into one teaching. His eclecticism and syncretism anticipated the distinctive direction in which Japanese Confucianism would develop during the Tokugawa period. Orthodox and heterodox strains of Confucianism played equally important roles in the intellectual and spiritual lives of Tokugawa Confucians.[12]

Moreover, while most Korean and Chinese Confucians of the time were stringently opposed to mixing Confucian spirituality with Buddhist, Daoist, or popular religious practices, some seventeenth-century Japanese Confucians such as Nakae Tōju freely invoked theistic Shintō terminology and imagery, describing the human mind as "the divine light... before

Figure 3.4. Portrait of Nakae Tōju depicting distinctive chonmage hairstyle of elite Tokugawa period men. Source: Wikimedia Commons, Reggaeman, http://upload.wikimedia.org/wikipedia/commons/8/8c/Nakae_Toju_portrait.jpg.

which one stands as if in a mirror, with nothing hidden either good or bad…. [Human beings] are all gifted with the divine light that tells good from bad."[13] Nakae saw values such as filial piety in both conventional Confucian terms and as the divine legacy of Shintō deities. In this way, developments in Tokugawa Confucianism made it possible for Japanese, whether *samurai* or commoners, to understand their obedience to the state, respect for elders, performance of duties, pursuit of learning, and worship of *kami* as equal expressions of Confucian piety and self-cultivation.

CONFUCIANISM AND JAPANESE SOCIETY

By 1790, Zhu Xi's version of Confucianism was the official ideology of the Tokugawa state. All aspects of Japanese social life were impacted by Confucian ideas, institutions, and practices. While the emperor still ruled in name, real control was in the hands of the *shōgun* and his feudal lords. Tokugawa society was organized according to a fourfold hierarchy, with *samurai* at the top, peasants followed by artisans in the middle, and merchants at the bottom. As *samurai* became anachronisms living on fixed incomes during the peaceful if authoritarian period of Tokugawa rule, their hereditary status increasingly contrasted with their economic status, while the opposite occurred with regard to merchants, who became both numerous and prosperous but still were subject to restrictive laws that prevented them from conspicuously displaying their wealth. Despite or perhaps because of the low place assigned to them in the Confucian social hierarchy, many merchants embraced Confucianism and even established their own state-chartered Confucian academy in the commercial metropolis of Osaka, which eventually led to merchant-scholars' claim that cosmic pattern could be discerned in market economics. Codes written by Tokugawa merchants for the instruction of their employees and heirs included Confucian mandates to obey the state and protect their household's reputation.

All levels of Tokugawa society gradually gained access to literacy through a nationwide network of Confucian educational institutions, the

Figure 3.5 Shizutani Gakkō, Bizen, Okayama prefecture, Japan. Source: Wikimedia Commons, scarletgreen, http://upload.wikimedia.org/wikipedia/commons/3/3b/Shizutani_school_10d.jpg.

本　籍	○○市○○町○T目○番地○○
氏　名	○○　○○
戸籍事項 戸籍編製	[改製日] 平成○○年○月○日 [改製事由] 平成6年法務省令第51号附則第2条第1項による改製
戸籍に記録されている者	[名] ○○ [生年月日] 昭和○○年○月○日　　　　　[配偶者区分] 夫 [父] ○○○○ [母] ○○○○ [続柄] 長男
身分事項 　出　生 　婚　姻	[出生日] 昭和○○年○月○日 [出生地] ○○市 [届出日] 昭和○○年○月○日 [届出人] 父 [婚姻日] 平成○○年○月○日 [配偶者氏名] ○○○○ [従前戸籍] ○○市○○町○T目○番○号　　　○○○○
戸籍に記録されている者	[名] ○○ [生年月日] 昭和○○年○月○日　　　　　[配偶者区分] 妻 [父] ○○○○ [母] ○○○○ [続柄] 次女
身分事項 　出　生 　婚　姻	[出生日] 昭和○○年○月○日 [出生地] ○○市○○区 [届出日] 昭和○○年○月○日 [届出人] 父 [婚姻日] 平成○○年○月○日 [配偶者氏名] ○○○○ [従前戸籍] ○○市○○区○○町○番地　　　○○○○

以下余白

これは、戸籍に記載されている事項の全部を証明した書面である。

平成○○年○月○日
　　○○市長　　○　○　　○　○

公印

Figure 3.6. Japanese family register (*koseki*). Source: Wikimedia Commons, Wakamin, http://upload.wikimedia.org/wikipedia/commons/1/10/Koseki-syoumei.jpg.

foremost of which was the Yushima Seidō (Sage Hall) in the capital of Edo (later renamed Tōkyō), which began as the private Confucian temple of Fujiwara Seika's disciple, Hayashi Razan. It became the premier state-supported Confucian institution in 1797, where the bureaucrats of the Tokugawa regime received their training. Far more influential in the lives of ordinary people, however, were institutions such as Japan's first public school, the Shizutani Gakkō ("Peaceful Valley School"), founded in 1666 by Ikeda Mitsumasa, the feudal lord of what now is Okayama prefecture on the island of Honshū. As a result of institutions at both the local and national levels, ordinary Japanese were indoctrinated in Confucian values. Law enforcement, mandatory registration at Buddhist temples, social conservatism, and the highly ritualized nature of everyday life also worked together to produce a social atmosphere of rigid hierarchy and effective authoritarian rule.

Many observers of contemporary Japan trace the formality, reserve, and group-spiritedness of its so-called "shame culture" back to the nationwide Confucian socialization accomplished during the Tokugawa period. A great deal of this Confucian influence goes unacknowledged as such, given the closely interwoven tapestry of Confucianism, Buddhism, and Shintō that characterized Japanese religious culture. Examples abound. It was during the Tokugawa period that Buddhist altars, still found in most Japanese homes, became the place to keep ancestral tablets and therefore a venue of Confucian ancestor worship. Family registers (*koseki*), originally required by the Tokugawa state as a way to police registration at local Buddhist temples, still are maintained by each Japanese household. Loyalty to one's superiors, once conceptualized in terms of feudal relationships, now is expressed toward one's employer. Until Japan's recent economic disturbances, such loyalty was rewarded with lifetime employment. Within corporate organizations, schools, and families, it is customary to distinguish between one's *senpai*—those senior in rank or experience—and one's *kōhai*—those junior in rank or experience. The decision-making process known as *nemawashi*, "going around the roots," is typical of how changes ideally occur in Japanese families, groups, and organizations. This process entails careful and discreet consultation with others, gradually and quietly building consensus until the proposed change can be implemented with a minimum of discomfort. Finally, instead of a Chinese- or Korean-style civil service examination system, modern Japan has its *juken jigoku*, or "examination hell," an arduous series of tests that the majority of candidates for high school admissions work hard to pass in hopes of entering a high-ranked high school. The term "hell" may connote Buddhism, but the nature of the experience that it describes is purely Confucian, and every winter, aspiring students all over Japan seek the assistance of famous Confucian scholars who have been deified as *kami*, including Confucius himself, at Shintō shrines.

Despite the generally successful efforts of the Tokugawa state and Confucian institutions to promote the uniform Confucianization of Japanese society, perfect adherence to filial piety, loyalty to superiors, and disciplined self-cultivation was more often ideal than real. Near the end

Figure 3.7. Portrait of Sugiwara no Michizane (845–903) by
Kikuchi Yōsai (1781–1878). Mihizane has been deified as
Tenjin, the patron kami of scholarship. Source: Wikimedia
Commons, http://upload.wikimedia.org/wikipedia/
commons/8/87/Sugawara_Michizane.jpg.

of his life, a nineteenth-century *samurai*, Katsu Kokichi, wrote a memoir
intended to guide future generations not by his personal example, but rather
through his reflections on his failure to live up to Confucian expectations:

> I indulged in every manner of folly and nonsense in my
> lifetime.... Only recently have I come to my sense and begun
> to act more like a human being. When I think of my past,

my hair stands on end.... Even putting these words on paper fills me with shame.... I will never know how much anguish I caused my relatives, parents, wife, and children. Even more reprehensible, I behaved most disloyally to my lord and master the shogun and with uttermost defiance to my superiors.... My past conduct truly fills me with horror.[14]

CONFUCIANISM AND THE JAPANESE STATE

Japan in the early twentieth century may be the best example of a modern Confucian empire. As the Tokugawa order collapsed in the face of Western challenges, Japan's new rulers united under the banner of the emperor Meiji, who was "restored" to power in 1868 after the surrender and resignation of the final Tokugawa *shōgun*. Although some early Meiji reformers questioned the value of Confucian traditions, especially in the arena of public education, by the late 1880s advocates of Confucian ideas succeeded in making Confucianism the foundation of Japan's new social and political order. The imperial regime used Confucian ideology to promote the image of the ruler as the father of the "family state" to whom all his subjects owed filial obedience and respect. In 1890, the Meiji state promulgated its *Imperial Rescript on Education*, which became required reading in Japanese schools and even the centerpiece of public rituals in which subjects pledged allegiance to the emperor. The text reads, in part: "Subjects, be filial to your parents, affectionate to your brothers and sisters; as husbands and wives be harmonious, as friends true; bear yourselves in modesty and moderation; extend your benevolence to all." The Confucian concept of the emperor as national parent gained strength from Shintō, which became the Meiji state religion and promoted the worship of the emperor as a god.

The merger of Confucianism and nationalism was not new with Japan, of course. Since the time of Confucius himself, Confucians have tended toward ethnocentrism, at least as far as reverence for the Chinese classics was concerned, even if the most profound expressions of the tradition aimed beyond clan and nation to a broader human allegiance. Developments in Japanese Confucianism near the end of the Tokugawa period helped prepare the way for the Meiji state's adaptation of Confucian ideology for nationalist purposes. During the eighteenth and ninteenth centuries, a Confucian movement known as *Kokugaku* ("National Studies") became popular. National Studies scholars resisted the idea of dependence upon Chinese learning and turned to Japanese history and literature for Confucian inspiration. Ultimately, one lesson learned by National

Figure 3.8. Portrait of Emperor Meiji (r. 1867–1912) surrounded by his divine and imperial ancestors (Chikanobu Toyohara, 1878). Source: Wikimedia Commons, http://upload.wikimedia.org/wikipedia/commons/6/69/Meiji-tenno_among_kami_and_emperors.JPG.

Studies scholars helped lead to the undoing of the Tokugawa *shōgun*: unlike Chinese or Korean history, Japanese history—as mythologized in Confucian-style texts such as the *Kojiki* and *Nihongi*—depicted one long, uninterrupted imperial dynasty from antiquity to the present. From a Confucian perspective, this suggested that Japan's emperors never lost the mandate of Heaven, unlike their Chinese and Korean counterparts, who rose and fall in dynastic waves over time. While not all Japanese Confucians supported National Studies, the combination of Confucianism and nationalism proved irresistible to all but a few. Chanting the slogan *sonnō jōi* ("revere the emperor, expel the barbarians"), Confucian scholars joined forces with those who wished to both restore imperial rule and repel Western influence.

The extension of Japanese power into Korea, Manchuria, Taiwan, and other Asian regions brought with it the expansion of Confucian traditions, albeit in forms designed to serve Japanese imperial interests, such as propagating the *Imperial Rescript* among Japan's colonial subjects. This Confucian rhetoric of empire persisted and intensified after the Meiji emperor's reign well into the 1930s and 1940s, when right-wing nationalist elements in Japanese politics gained the upper hand and led Japan into a disastrous war of conquest that aimed to bring all Western Pacific nations into a harmonious Greater East Asia Co-Prosperity Sphere. The links between Confucianism and imperialism in Japan were severed when Japan surrendered to the Allies in August 1945 following the atomic bombing of the cities of Hiroshima and Nagasaki. In the aftermath of the war, the United States occupational administration forced Japan's emperor to renounce his religious status, and the Japanese state was forbidden to establish any religious tradition, Confucian or otherwise, as its official ideology.

The post-World War Two era has witnessed both the twilight of Confucianism as an institutional force in Japanese culture and its alleged rebirth as the driving ideology of national economic and social recovery. The rapid economic development that followed Japan's defeat and occupation, especially during the 1960s, was attributed by some observers to Japan's Confucian capacity for deferred gratification, selfless dedication to group welfare, and phenomenally efficient organizational structure. At the same time, the selective Westernization of Japanese society seemed quite intense. Nonetheless, the generation that governed postwar Japan, taught in its schools and universities, and ran its corporations was the generation that came of age during the peak of Japan's right-wing Confucian-Shintō phase, and members of this older generation remained confident that a more benign version of these values continued to guide the nation. American journalist Frank Gibney reported a conversation that he once had with a Japanese businessman:

> [A]n old Japanese friend and business partner, driving back to Chicago with me after a festive golf-and-dinner Sunday in the suburbs, offered me some insight into the soul of his nation. "You know," he confided, patting one of his new graphite golf clubs, "you can forget about talk of Buddhism or Shinto or any other religion with us. It's just Confucianism. That's what we're all about."[15]

This conversation took place during the late 1970s, when Japan's postwar boom was nearly at its height, and before public anguish about failing corporations, degenerate youth, and low birthrates began to dominate Japanese media. After the collapse of Japan's hyper-expansive "bubble economy" in 1990, followed by the 1997 Asian financial crisis and the global economic catastrophe of 2008, Japan's rapidly aging population, diminishing numbers of women marrying and having children, affluent young pleasure-seekers, and disappearing agricultural sector were interpreted as signs of imminent doom, even though many European nations share all of these characteristics but don't seem to have Japan's sense of alarm. One characteristic that Japan does not share with its European counterparts is its Confucian heritage, which may prove to

Figure 3.9. Sign explaining pandemic protocols in a Japanese convenience store, April 11, 2020. Source: Wikimedia Commons, KKPCW, https://upload. wikimedia.org/wikipedia/commons/b/b2/Request_of_Social_distance_for_ protecting_from_infecting_Covid-19_by_procession.jpg.

be the factor that enables the Japanese to survive and even thrive amidst the transformations of globalization. And yet Confucianism's future prospects in Japan, like its history in the archipelago, are complicated. On the one hand, Confucian deference to authority and conformity with social norms have been credited with helping Japan to escape the worst excesses of the COVID-19 pandemic through near-universal compliance with mask-wearing and social distancing directives not seen in many other countries. On the other hand, the Confucian tradition of achieving social order through the "soft power" of community spirit rather than the "hard power" of government legislation may be blamed for Japan's slow progress toward vaccination in comparison with other nations. Moving forward, Confucianism may be both an asset and a liability for an ever-changing Japan.

4

CONFUCIANISM IN VIỆT NAM

In June 2021, the Communist government of Việt Nam introduced a new social media "code of conduct" for the nation. Home to the world's seventh largest social media user base, Việt Nam is a country that now expects those who use Facebook, TikTok, and other social media to "promote the beauty of Việt Nam's scenery, people and culture, and spread good stories about good people." The new expectations also forbid the use of vulgar language or content that threatens or questions "the interests of the state."[1] While this policy of self-censorship likely is unenforceable and arose from authoritarian paranoia rather than Confucian concerns, one may see within it an echo of traditional Confucian values: a professed faith in ordinary people's capacity to regulate themselves morally for the public good, an implicit ethnocentrism and cultural nationalism that celebrates the shared community, and an earnest appeal to public exemplars as a way of shaping the national conscience.

Such lingering public gestures in the direction of Confucianism, however vague, are reminders that, like their Chinese neighbors, Việt Nam's Communist rulers are turning to traditional cultural resources—not only to bolster their own grip on power, but also to cope with the rapid social changes wrought by record increases in Gross Domestic Product, exports, and tourism, as well as the globalizing and modernizing pressures that accompany such rapid economic development. Only a generation or so after the devastating "American War" that brought decades of political and social division to a decisive, if brutal, end, Việt Nam remains a country with more than one thousand years of strong Confucian tradition. This abiding tradition may be seen in seemingly-ancient sites and festivals that actually are of recent invention, such as Việt Nam's National Poetry Day, an immensely popular festival celebrated annually at Hanoi's Confucian temple (*Văn Miếu*) beginning in 2003. Like the festival, the temple appears ancient and has been in use for almost a thousand years, but it actually

Figure 4.1. Pavilion containing memorial slabs (atop stone tortoise, center) commemorating Confucian scholars at a Confucian temple, Hanoi, Việt Nam. Source: Wikimedia Commons, audrey_sel, http://upload.wikimedia.org/wikipedia/commons/5/5b/Temple_of_ Literature_1.jpg.

contains much that is modern, since it was partially reconstructed at state expense in 2000. The largest and most important of several Confucian temples established as part of the national civil service examination system implemented by King Lý Thánh Tông (r. 1054–1072) and his successors and the home of the Imperial Confucian Academy, Việt Nam's oldest educational institution, it is an almost-exact replica of the Confucian temple in Confucius' hometown of Qufu in China's Shandong province. On National Poetry Day, one must contend with surging crowds to pass from the temple courtyard through a series of gates entitled, successively, "Great Center," "Attained Talent," and "Accomplished Virtue," in order to reach the "Well of Heavenly Clarity," where eighty-two stone slabs list more than 1,300 successful imperial examination candidates by their names and hometowns. Amidst these monuments as well as altars to Confucius, King Lý Nhân Tông, and other sages of antiquity, quotations from Confucian texts are inscribed on silk banners, attached to huge red balloons, and released into the air to rise to the heavens.[2] This display of Confucian piety demonstrates the abiding reverence for history, learning, and literature among the people of Việt Nam, where Confucianism has a history almost as long as that of Chinese Confucianism

THE ORIGINS OF CONFUCIANISM IN VIỆT NAM

In Việt Nam, Confucianism is not seen as a Chinese tradition, but rather as a native expression of Vietnamese values. Việt Nam has chafed against being lumped together with China for most of its more than two-thousand-year history. The roots of Vietnamese nationhood lie in the ancient states of Văn Lang and Âu Lạc, formed in what now is northern Việt Nam and China's southern Guangxi province between the seventh and third centuries BCE.[3] By 179 BCE, Âu Lạc (which had come to include Văn Lang) was annexed by the Nam Việt (Chinese *Nan Yue*) kingdom founded by the Chinese general, Zhao Tuo, a former Qin dynasty official, which extended to what now is the Chinese city of Guangzhou, north of Hong Kong. Nam Việt became a vassal state of China's Han dynasty, which struggled to impose obedience until its defeat of the revolt led by two sisters, Trưng Trắc and Trưng Nhị, who committed suicide rather than surrender to Chinese forces in 43 CE. After the deaths of the Trưng sisters and their rebel movement, Chinese regimes dominated the Vietnamese region until 938 CE, although uprisings (often led by women, just as in the case of the Trưng sisters) occurred periodically. The inclusion of the Vietnamese people in first millennium China's zone of cultural influence

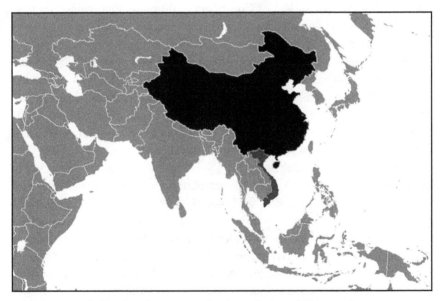

Map 4.1. Map indicating the present-day boundaries of China and Việt Nam. Source: Wikimedia Commons, User: Circeus, http://upload. wikimedia.org/wikipedia/commons/7/77/People%27s_Republic_of_ China_Vietnam_Locator.png.

and political control meant that Vietnamese elites received Confucian educations, trained for service in China's imperial bureaucracy, and adopted Chinese customs, especially with regard to Confucian arenas such as marriage rites, family structure, and literary expression. By the tenth century, when Việt Nam gained its independence from Chinese rule, its culture had shed many of its apparently matriarchal qualities and had become deeply Chinese in many ways, even though a fierce sense of nationalism dominated its relationship with China. The "Chinese-ness" of medieval Vietnamese culture expressed itself partially in Confucian terms, but mostly in terms of two other traditions imported from China: Daoism and especially Buddhism.

In 938, the Vietnamese commander Ngô Quyền, the son of a former Vietnamese official of China's Tang dynasty, repelled a Chinese force sent to establish control over northern Việt Nam and seized power as the first king of the new Đại Việt state, ruling from the former Âu Lạc capital of Cổ Loa. Vietnamese Buddhists were in a better position than Vietnamese Confucians to influence the newly-independent nation, as most Vietnamese Confucians had been dispatched to serve as officials in China, while Vietnamese who became Buddhist monks and nuns remained in their home country. Just as in Korea and Japan, it was Buddhist institutions that transmitted a great deal of Confucian tradition to Vietnamese society, even though Buddhism clearly subordinated Confucianism and other rival traditions to itself.[4] As the reign of Ngô Quyền gave way to the short-lived Đinh and Early Lê dynasties during the tenth century, Confucians became more important to securing the stability of Đại Việt. Founded in 1009, the Lý dynasty adopted many Confucian ideas, institutions, and practices in order to shore up its authority, including a Confucian-style civil service examination system, hierarchy of official ranks, and centralized government control of agricultural production, even though its official religion was Buddhism. King Lý Thánh Tông received a Confucian education and later sponsored the construction of the aforementioned Confucian temple in what now is Hanoi. By 1198, Vietnamese Confucians felt sufficiently empowered to pressure the Lý ruler to reduce the number of Buddhist monks in the country. However, after the fall of the Lý dynasty and the rise of the Trần dynasty, which renewed ties between Việt Nam's rulers and Buddhism, Confucians found themselves unable to serve in high government positions and began to openly resist Buddhist influence in elite circles and national affairs. In the fourteenth century, the Confucian scholar Trương Hán Siêu participated in the dedication of a Buddhist temple by calling for the banning of Buddhism and the restoration of Confucianism:

> Superstitious beliefs [i.e., Buddhism] must be banned while the
> Saint's way [i.e., Confucianism] has to be restored.[5]

The overthrow of the Trần dynasty by the Confucian-minded Ho Qui Ly brought renewed government support to the tradition, but at a cost. Ho had his own ideas about what constituted Confucianism, elevating the Duke of Zhou above Confucius in the pantheon of Confucian saints and publishing criticisms of the most orthodox Song dynasty "Neo-Confucian," Zhu Xi.[6] This brief flowering of a distinctively Vietnamese Confucianism was brought to a sudden end by invading Ming dynasty forces in 1407, which toppled Ho's regime and began a program of forced Confucianization along conventional Chinese lines in Đại Việt. Confident of its "civilizing mission" in Việt Nam, the Ming government established local Confucian temples and schools in every district, mandated the wearing of Chinese-style apparel, and distributed Confucian texts by the cartload. While the heavy hand of Chinese colonialism eventually spurred the Vietnamese to rebel and reclaim their independence, it also established a deeply Confucian foundation for the development of Vietnamese traditions of self-cultivation.

CONFUCIANISM AND VIETNAMESE SELF-CULTIVATION

The architects of Vietnamese revolt against Ming dynasty rule rejected Chinese domination but not Confucianism. The founder of the Lê Dynasty, Lê Lợi (r. 1428–1433), proclaimed Việt Nam's status as a civilized empire independent of China while implementing Confucian-style measures—such as reinstituting the civil service examination system—to restore stability and order. His successors were even more ardently devoted to Confucianism, and by the 1470s, only those who married according to strict Confucian ritual could receive appointment or promotion as government officials, and state-sponsored texts explaining Confucian morality were required reading for Lê subjects. The interruption of Lê rule during the sixteenth century by the usurping Mạc dynasty, supporters of Ming China and descendants of fourteenth-century Vietnamese Confucian scholars, only intensified the steady Confucianization of Vietnamese society. Once the Lê dynasty was reestablished in 1593, government promotion of Confucianism extended to the public recognition of filial sons, chaste widows, and exemplary students, which entailed not only the bestowal of commemorative plaques by the Lê emperor but also exemption from the forced labor periodically required of most commoners.

Figure 4.2. Statue of Lê Lợi in front of City Hall, Thanh Hóa, Việt Nam. Note the receptacle for incense offerings. Source: Wikimedia Commons, Nguyễn Thanh Quang, http://upload.wikimedia.org/wikipedia/commons/8/81/Le_Loi_statue.JPG.

Like its counterparts in Chŏson Korea and Ming China, Confucianism in Lê Việt Nam was under the sway of the Song dynasty master Zhu Xi and his school of thought. Confucian scholars in Việt Nam rarely departed from such "Neo-Confucian" interpretations of classical Chinese texts, which were printed, distributed, studied, and taught at government expense as well as translated into *chữ nôm* (the vernacular script developed during the tenth century). Although official texts continued to be composed in classical Chinese, by the eighteenth century, Confucian-themed literature written in chữ nôm had become commonplace, and the Lê government briefly adopted *chữ nôm* as the nation's official script. Confucian writings in *chữ nôm* tended toward moralistic themes and generally served to extend elite values across Việt Nam's increasingly multi-ethnic empire, since even the illiterate were introduced to *chữ nôm* texts through oral performance at the local village level. Vernacular texts such as the *Gia Huan Ca (Family Training Ode)*, which began to circulate during the 1400s and gradually became part of popular oral tradition, have a deeply Confucian flavor:

> Achieving a reputation brings good fortune from Heaven for
> 10,000 generations. . . .
> We must persevere in being filial night and day.
> Because affection arises, [our elders] frequently reprimand,
> Wanting us to correct our faults and become better people.
> Carefully and circumspectly,
> Record in your heart and soul parental words which are worthy
> of being engraved therein.[7]

Although such literature might be seen as a vehicle for purely Chinese values, it also helped to create a distinctively Vietnamese Confucianism that transformed traditional Chinese practices—such as the meticulous writing of history to record moral examples—into ways of nurturing an independent Vietnamese consciousness, such as paying careful attention to Việt Nam's past as a Chinese colony in order to prevent future invasions by China. In the absence of widespread access to formal schooling, theatrical performances often functioned as institutions of moral education. Popular plays dramatized the conflicts that could arise within the five relationships defined by Confucian morality (ruler-subject, father-son, husband-wife, elder sibling-younger sibling, and friend-friend) and promoted Confucian values in the resolution of these conflicts. The operatic theatrical tradition known as *hát tuồng* or *hát bội*, still performed in contemporary Việt Nam, preserves such Confucian elements through its reliance on historical narratives and stock moralistic characters. In these ways, Vietnamese poets and playwrights both perpetuated Confucian ideas, institutions, and practices found across East Asia and worked to build a cultural identity separate from China.

The literary path to Confucian self-cultivation also was encouraged by emperor Lê Thánh Tông (r. 1460–1497). A serious student of Confucianism as a youth, he embraced "Neo-Confucian" teachings and, once in power, reinvigorated the Confucian civil service examination system, which enabled a new meritocratic elite to replace the entrenched oligarchy. By his order, Confucian temples were established in every province, and the construction of new Buddhist and Daoist institutions was suspended. Under Lê Thánh Tông's rule, Vietnamese Confucianism took on a populist flavor and became associated with political reform and social mobility, even though it also enforced a strict social hierarchy in which members of various classes were clearly differentiated by a mandatory dress code. Social status and personal honor came to depend upon the perception of an individual's *duc* (moral virtue), which could be cultivated by submitting to Confucian traditions of education, filiality, and government service.

Despite the Lê dynasty's embrace of Confucianism and its subsequent empowerment as an institution, Buddhism and Daoism remained powerful influences on Vietnamese beliefs about human potential and spiritual pursuits. In the popular concept of *so* (personal destiny), which still influences Vietnamese life today, what might be called "Chinese" or "Confucian" traditions of collective belonging and what might be called "Vietnamese" or "Buddhist" and "Daoist" notions of individual free will came to intersect. *So* is regarded as the combined result of both one's individual karma and the moral merit of one's ancestors, as well as impersonal shifts in the cosmic cycle of *yin* and *yang*. Virtuous female ancestors are seen as the key to attaining moral merit in this lifetime, and conversely women of high moral character can assume that their descendants will enjoy good fortune. At the same time, one's fate can be altered for the better by acts of individual will, such as the renunciation of material comforts for the sake of moral purpose or the pursuit of moral education. Thus, one is both responsible for one's own moral progress and accountable to both one's ancestors and one's descendants insofar as karmic legacies are concerned. This cluster of concepts and practices has produced a uniquely Vietnamese vision of self-cultivation that blends Confucian notions of filial piety and moral perfectibility with the Buddhist theory of karmic retribution and Daoist cosmology. Lê Thánh Tông himself, although revered as one of Việt Nam's greatest rulers, can be regarded as both the moral heir of his virtuous forebears and as a paragon of personal rectitude, who in turn bequeathed to his descendants a legacy of formidable merit.

CONFUCIANISM AND VIETNAMESE SOCIETY

The reign of Lê Thánh Tông introduced new laws that both shaped Vietnamese society according to Chinese traditions and allowed for the preservation of distinctive national customs, especially with regard to

Figure 4.3. Portrait of Lê Thánh Tông as ancestor, as displayed in Lê imperial family temple. Source: Wikimedia Commons, không rõ, http://upload.wikimedia.org/ wikipedia/commons/f/f6/206ThoiLe_LeThanhTong.jpg.

the treatment of women and the relationship of the individual to his or her larger family. While these Confucian-inspired laws did not succeed in transforming the Vietnamese state into a wholly Confucian-identified institution, as was the case in Song dynasty China or Chosŏn Korea, they did help to establish both Confucian values and a distinctively Vietnamese identity at the more fundamental level of popular social norms.

In China during the Song dynasty and afterward, multi-generational families sharing the same household represented the Confucian social norm. Marriage required parental consent, family property was inherited by men only, and women who divorced or outlived their husbands could not claim their former or deceased husbands' goods. A woman was expected to be subordinate to male authority throughout her lifetime: her father during childhood, her husband during marriage, and her son during widowhood. In contrast, the Lê legal code did not require parental consent for marriage and granted equal inheritance rights to female as well as male heirs. Unlike the model Chinese Confucian family, the Vietnamese norm was a smaller social unit that might live apart from the home of the household head's parents, even if they still were alive. Chinese families were patrilineal (tracing ancestry through male lineages) and patrilocal (establishing households in the husband's family home), whereas traditional Vietnamese families were led by strong women, known as *noi tuong* ("generals of the within"). Popular texts such as the *Family Training Ode* credit women as the source of their children's moral virtue, and female ancestors still enjoy considerable ritual attention in present-day Vietnamese life. Perhaps in recognition of women's relatively greater status and power in Vietnamese society, Lê law stipulated that women retained both their individual property after their marriages were dissolved by divorce or death, and divided property acquired during marriage equally between both divorced spouses and between a remarried widow and her deceased husband's family.

Despite the rights and responsibilities granted to women in Lê Việt Nam, the central Confucian institution of the family remained paramount in importance. Village society was built on blood relationships between fellow residents of a particular locale, and many village names reflect the blood ties that bind together such communities by consisting of a clan name followed by the term *Xá*, meaning "place"—for example, the village of Mai Xá ("place of the Mai clan") in modern Quảng Trị province, which is associated with a longstanding Confucian tradition in north central Việt Nam. The interrelated members of village communities defined their relationships with one another in terms of a nine-fold generational scheme, and traditional Vietnamese language developed a variety of pronouns and honorific terms in order to express deference to others' seniority in the multi-generational social world of village life. All members of village society were expected to participate in the Confucian veneration of ancestors, since most villagers shared a common ancestry with their neighbors.

Figure 4.4. Altar with offerings to ancestors displayed during Tết (lunar New Year) in a north Vietnamese home. Source: Wikimedia Commons, cadzo, http://upload. wikimedia.org/wikipedia/commons/0/06/Ancestors_Altar_or_Gods_Altar_in_ Tet%2C_North_Vietnam.jpg.

Confucian ancestor ritual in Việt Nam, like its counterparts elsewhere in East Asia, includes many Buddhist and Daoist elements, but ultimately is based upon classically Confucian concerns for the harmonious maintenance of human relationships across generations and beyond the grave. Most Vietnamese households still maintain a family altar at which candles, incense, food, and flowers may be offered to honor the ancestors whose names are inscribed on the family genealogical tablet, both on a regular basis and on specific occasions, such as ancestors' death anniversaries, *Tết* (lunar New Year), and "Piety Day" (observed during the seventh month of the traditional lunar calendar). The tradition of honoring the foremost ancestor of the Confucian tradition itself, Confucius, goes back to 1156, when the first Confucian worship hall in Việt Nam was built. As is the case in other East Asian countries, Vietnamese celebrate the birthday of Confucius on the twenty-eighth day of the ninth month in the traditional lunar calendar (typically observed in late September or early October). This ritual may be observed today at the Confucian temple located in what now is the Zoo and Botanical Gardens in Hồ Chí Minh City (formerly known as Saigon).

By the 1600s, a cultural gap between Việt Nam's southern and northern regions had emerged. While the north maintained fidelity to Confucian traditions, the south leaned more heavily on Buddhism as a source of social values. As a cosmopolitan, international religion, Buddhism naturally lent itself to the assimilation and adaptation of multiple ethnic traditions, such as the cult of goddesses worshiped by the Cham, a people who live in what now are Cambodia and Thailand as well as Việt Nam. Perhaps because of its greater proximity to China, northern Việt Nam remained more rigidly committed to Confucian social hierarchies, while the relaxation of Confucian orthodoxy in the south enabled a newfound social mobility to develop there. Northern Vietnamese Confucians responded by promoting a pejorative view of the south as a region that was not truly "Vietnamese," even though many Confucian values embraced in the north actually were Chinese in origin. In 1663, the Lê government issued a proclamation from its capital in the north that called upon all of its subjects to reform society along Confucian lines by demanding children's subordination to parents, wives' subordination to husbands, and the living's subordination to the dead in the form of officially-worshiped ancestors. This proclamation did little to reconcile the growing cultural and regional divisions in the country or to revive the dynasty's sagging legitimacy.

The tensions between Chinese and Vietnamese social values and between Chinese and Vietnamese claims to cultural ownership of Confucianism make it difficult to accept the commonplace claim that "for ten centuries Confucianism was the intellectual and ideological backbone of [Việt Nam]."[8] At the same time, no one can deny that by the beginning of the Nguyen dynasty in 1802, Vietnamese society had been profoundly shaped by Confucian traditions and to a large extent was defined by those traditions, even if Vietnamese Confucianism was not as strongly identified with its state version as was its Chinese counterpart. This distinctively Vietnamese Confucian identity may be seen in the writings of Trương Tửu, a twentieth-century Vietnamese intellectual who argued that Việt Nam had an equal claim with China to having produced classical Confucian literature of lasting value:

> [W]e [Vietnamese] also have precious canonical Odes (*Kinh thi*) that are no less worthy than the Odes [*Shijing*] of the Chinese. Our duty today is to write them down, ensure their accuracy, and annotate them, as the Duke of Zhou wrote down, Confucius ensured the accuracy, and Zhu Xi annotated the Odes of China.... [W]e can do it....[9]

CONFUCIANISM AND THE VIETNAMESE STATE

The successors of Lê Thánh Tông were neither as powerful nor as popular as he, and from the 1500s through the 1700s, the real rulers of Việt Nam were the aristocratic military leaders of the Trịnh clan who dominated the later Lê throne in much the same way that *shōguns* controlled Japan from the thirteenth through the nineteenth centuries. After a brief period of peasant rebellions and civil unrest between 1770 and 1802, during which the Lê emperor sought shelter in Qing dynasty China, the lords of the Nguyễn clan seized power and inaugurated Việt Nam's final imperial dynasty. It was during the period of Nguyễn rule that Việt Nam acquired its modern name, but it also was during this time that Chinese-style Confucianism was imposed most aggressively by the state.

The Nguyễn dynasty abandoned the Lê strategy of compromise between indigenous and imported Confucian norms and ordered the wholesale implementation of the legal code promulgated by China's Qing regime. Despite the institution of new penalties for "unfilial" offenses, such as establishing an independent household during the lifetime of one's parents or granting inheritance to divorcées and widows (both tolerated and even affirmed by Lê law), the Nguyễn's attempt to introduce a more orthodox—that is, more Chinese—version of Confucianism did not lead to significant changes in Vietnamese social practices. It did establish the state as the primary purveyor of Confucian values in Vietnamese society.

Nguyễn state funds subsidized study for the imperial civil service examinations and the writing of academic commentaries on Confucian classics, rewarded public exemplars of Confucian morality, and paid for the construction of Confucian temples throughout the realm. Copies of the *Classic of Changes* translated into *chữ nôm* were printed at government expense in order to help those who lacked literacy in classical Chinese to memorize the text. Nguyễn Confucians generally prided themselves on having maintained an unbroken intellectual and spiritual lineage that went back to Confucius himself, often defending the Confucian tradition more fiercely than their Chinese counterparts. Some Nguyễn officials used their scholarly positions and literary connections to promote Confucianism and disparage Buddhism. Others preached the compatibility of Confucian and Buddhist teachings, as in Phan Huy Ích's commentary on the Trúc Lâm sect of Buddhism published in 1796:

> Although the teachings of [Buddhism]... state that everything
> is empty and immaterial, their main point is [to encourage
> people] to eliminate barriers and comprehend the suchness of

existence; to concentrate on clearing one's mind in order to discover one's true nature. In comparing this with... making one's intent sincere and extending one's knowledge, there is nothing here that is contradictory. I have heard that [Confucius] stated that "In the West there is a great sage." He therefore never denigrated [Buddhism] as heterodox.[10]

The Confucian identity of the Nguyễn state voiced itself most powerfully in response to the threats of French colonialism and Roman Catholic Christianity that emerged not long after the establishment of the dynasty. Emperor Minh Mạng (r. 1820–1841) was aware of both European encroachment and Christian missionaries and publicly commended the government of Edo period Japan for having expelled Europeans and banned Christianity. The collaboration of Lê loyalists with Catholic missionaries provided an excuse for both Nguyễn persecution of Christianity and French military involvement in Việt Nam, where troops were dispatched to protect missionaries and converts. France had maintained an interest in Việt Nam since the reign of Napoleon, and now reports of anti-Christian persecution emboldened advocates for the colonization of Việt Nam by France. By 1825, Minh Mạng had banned all Christian missionary activity in Việt Nam, and during the 1830s, seven missionaries who violated the ban were executed. Despite or perhaps because of the Confucian state's forceful repression of both Catholicism and rebel movements, resistance to Nguyễn rule and conversions to Catholicism only increased during the mid-nineteenth century.

In 1858, French naval forces arrived in order to punish the Nguyễn regime for its resistance to Catholic evangelism and to relations with European powers. By 1861, the naval expedition had become an all-out war, and three southern provinces surrendered in 1862 and became the French colony of Cochinchina, which in turn led to French domination of neighboring Cambodia and Laos. As more and more Vietnamese territory fell under French control, Vietnamese Catholics allied with the French were empowered and gained access to education, official employment, and estates that formerly belonged to the Nguyễn court. *Quốc ngữ*, a new script for writing the Vietnamese language developed by Catholic missionaries and based on Roman letters, was introduced and eventually became the official script of the French colonial administration. France's complete annexation of Việt Nam in 1887 reduced Nguyễn rule to the Annam region in central Việt Nam, now a French protectorate. The collapse of the Nguyễn state, the gradual replacement of both classical Chinese and *chữ nôm* (both of which were associated with Confucian literature) with

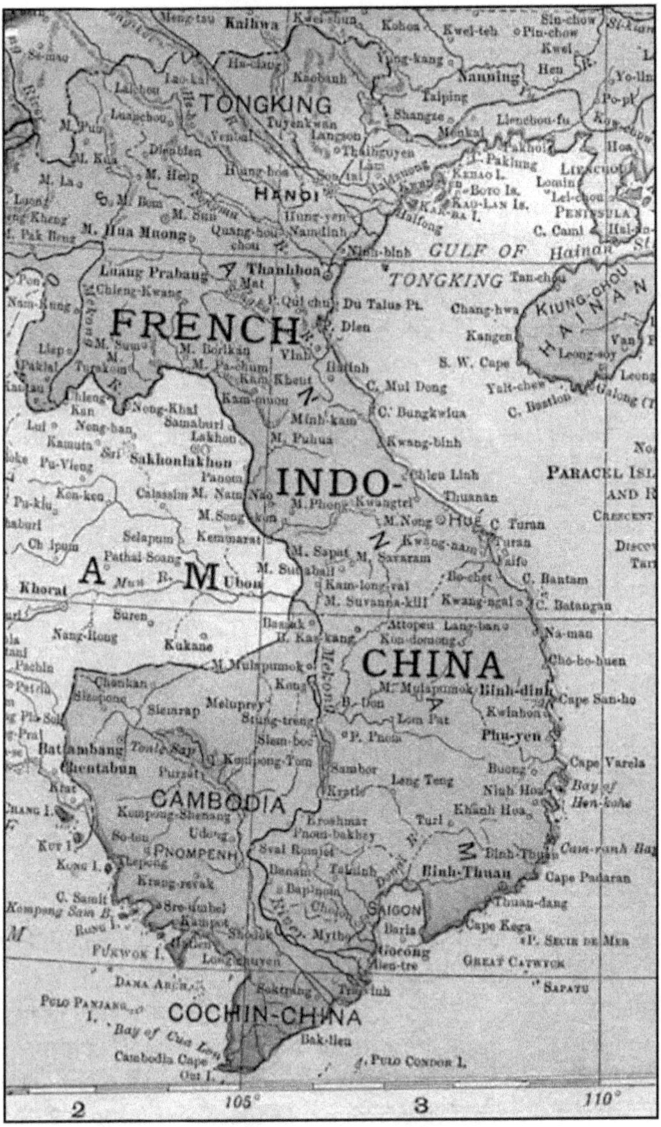

Map 4.2. Map of French colonial possessions in Southeast Asia, c. 1913. Source: Wikimedia Commons, http://en.wikipedia.org/wiki/ File:Indochine_fran%C3%A7aise_%281913%29.jpg.

quốc ngữ as the language of official and popular publications, and the introduction of Western learning hastened the demise of Confucianism as an institutional force in Vietnamese society. By the end of the nineteenth century, Vietnamese Confucianism was stripped of its traditional state support and seemed doomed to extinction.

In this atmosphere of decline, some Vietnamese Confucians maintained their defense of traditional values. The official and poet Nguyen Kyuyen wrote:

> If the world is becoming a new world,
> Public manners should nevertheless follow ancient models.
> I wake up in the morning to read the [*Classic of Changes*] alone.
> Understanding the change of times is no easy task.[11]

Others despaired. As the nineteenth century drew to a close, Le Van Ngu studied in France and was duly impressed by Western technology, but criticized his countrymen for abandoning their Confucian heritage in favor of European traditions, especially Christianity and industrialization, which he saw as destructive of all that Confucian teachings had nurtured in the Vietnamese people:

> [Vietnamese] should know that the wonder of the [*Classic of Changes*] was ten thousand times more amazing than Western principles of cannon, ship, car or electricity.... The Westerners came to the Eastern world by sea and brought us strange skills and playful things. Confused by and absorbed in Western learning, our people pursued fame and profit. The [*Classic of Changes*] became a bunch of wastepaper.... If people do not follow the great moral principle of benevolence and [do] not... control their desire to conquer, then more sophisticated mining will produce more natural resources. More natural resources cause more human desires. Human beings will become more difficult to live and then they go to invade others.[12]

Still other Vietnamese Confucians fought against French domination with more than words. Phan Đình Phùng, a Nguyễn official, was the descendant of twelve previous generations of Confucian scholars and imperial ministers. In exile after the death of his imperial patron, emperor Tự Đức, in 1883, Phan organized the first Vietnamese movement of armed resistance against colonial rule. Known as the *Cần Vương* ("Effort for the Ruler"), Phan's movement sought to replace Việt Nam's French overlords with the twelve-year-old Nguyễn heir. However, the young ruler soon was deposed by a coalition of French forces and Vietnamese rebels and spent the remainder of his life in exile under French rule. Undaunted, Phan took his resistance efforts underground, conducting guerilla warfare against the French colonial government and facing death many times. At one point, French troops desecrated Phan's ancestral tombs, publicly displayed his ancestors' remains, and threatened to kill his brother if he did not surrender. Phan responded to these actions by saying:

From the time I joined... the *Cần Vương* movement, I determined to forget the question of family and village. Now I have but one tomb, a very large one, that must be defended: the land of [Việt Nam]. I have only one brother, very important, that is in danger: more than twenty million countrymen. If I worry about my own tombs, who will worry about defending the tombs of the rest of the country? If I save my own brother, who will save all the other brothers of the country? ... If anyone carves up my brother, remember to send me some of the soup.[13]

Figure 4.5. Statue of Phan Đình Phùng in Hồ Chí Minh City (Saigon). Source: Wikimedia Commons, Amore Mio, http://upload.wikimedia.org/wikipedia/commons/9/9b/Statue_of_Phan_Dinh_Phung_2_crop.JPG.

Other modes of Vietnamese resistance to French domination expressed themselves in new ways while borrowing from Confucian and other East Asian traditions. The *Cao Đài* ("High Platform") religious movement, which combines Buddhist, Daoist, Confucian, and Christian elements, can be interpreted as a Vietnamese response to both religious domination by the West and the declining authority of traditional Vietnamese religions. According to Cao Đài teachings, one all-powerful God has spoken to humanity through a threefold historical process of revelation; God's messengers have included the Confucian sages Fuxi and Confucius as well as the Buddha, Laozi, and Jesus Christ, and Cao Đài saints include French figures such as Joan of Arc and Victor Hugo as well as the Chinese nationalist Sun Yat-sen. Between its inception in 1919 and the end of French rule in 1945, Cao Đài members actively opposed the colonial administration using both military and political means.

Wielding handmade grenades named in honor of Phan Đình Phùng, Vietnamese Communists led by Hồ Chí Minh (1890–1969) led the resistance against foreign occupiers—first against the Japanese in the 1940s, and then against the French throughout the 1950s. After Japan's defeat in August 1945, Communist and French forces contended for control of the country until 1954, when the Geneva Conference partitioned Việt Nam into a Communist north led by Hồ Chí Minh and a quasi-imperial south ruled by the last Nguyễn emperor, Bảo Đại (r. 1926–1945), who had collaborated with both the Japanese and the French and had officially abdicated when the Japanese surrendered. Bảo Đại's tenure as chief of state of South Việt Nam ended after only one year, when he was ousted by Ngô Đình Diệm, an anti-Communist official who claimed descent from both Confucian and Catholic forebears. Diệm claimed authority over all of Việt Nam and attempted to define Vietnamese nationalism in both anti-French and anti-Communist terms, seeking aid from the United States, which became increasingly involved in Việt Nam's civil war. Diệm's regime polarized the country, marginalized its Buddhist majority, and galvanized his Communist opposition.

Some of those associated with the Diệm government looked to Confucian traditions for help in guiding the divided nation back to unity and greatness. Tôn Thất Thiện, a descendant of a long line of Confucian scholars and Nguyễn officials whose marriage linked two of Việt Nam's leading Confucian families, served emperor Bảo Đại's Japanese-backed puppet government in mid-1945. After the fall of Bảo Đại's regime, he worked first for Hồ Chí Minh and then for Diệm. Although he was educated in England and Switzerland, Thiện sought to balance acknowledgement of

Western economic, political, and technological resources with affirmation of Việt Nam's Confucian heritage. This placed him at odds with both elements in the Diệm government who pushed a pro-Catholic, anti-traditional agenda and Hồ Chí Minh's Communists, who saw Confucianism as a symbol of the feudal social order that they aimed to destroy.

After Diệm's assassination by his own generals in 1963, Thiện left government service and became a journalist. In 1975, when it became clear that the Communist cause would be victorious, he exiled himself to Canada, from which he has continued to publish both scholarly and journalistic commentaries on Vietnamese affairs. Writing in 1980, after five years of unified rule by the Communist Party of Việt Nam, he pointed to the mass exodus of over 500,000 refugees who fled Việt Nam in the late 1970s, citing Confucian tradition: "As Mencius has said, when people decide to leave a country, it means that something is wrong with that country's government."[14]

The triumph of Việt Nam's Communists brought immediate and radical changes to the country. Communities associated with traditional Vietnamese culture, such as Buddhists, Confucians, and Daoists, as well as members of more recently-introduced religions, Christianity and Cao Đài, were lumped together as "lackeys of imperialism" by the Communist authorities. Representatives of these traditions faced enormous suspicion by government officials and were prominent among the million or so Vietnamese sent to re-education camps or otherwise harassed. Cao Đài was banned outright, and Christians experienced widespread persecution, especially among ethnic minority groups such as the Degar or Montagnards, who bear the stigma of having aided the U.S. Army during its support of the South Vietnamese government in the late 1960s and early 1970s. Vietnamese cultural leaders living outside of the country have lamented both the government's erosion of traditional culture and its manipulation of Vietnamese traditions to bolster its own legitimacy, especially in recent decades, as in the case of official sponsorship of National Poetry Day.

As Việt Nam has recovered from decades of war and unrest, the country has liberalized many economic policies, and its markets now are flooded with Western products and investments. Việt Nam's relations with the United States were normalized in 1995, and foreign producers of luxury goods now target the country as their next growth market. Recent census data indicates that up to eighty percent of the Vietnamese population participate in the combination of Buddhism, Confucianism, and Daoism known as Tam Đạo (the "Three Teachings"), and Marxist ideology appears to be fading away as Vietnamese youth become more familiar with Coca-Cola than Communism, although neither disillusionment with Marxism nor state endorsement of Confucianism appears to be as thorough in Việt Nam as each is in China. Nonetheless, although Hồ Chí Minh's face still appears on Vietnamese currency, the Confucian temple in Hanoi can be found on the reverse of the 100,000 *đồng* (worth approximately US$5) notes issued since 2003. It may be that the future of Việt Nam lies in a rediscovery and revival of its Confucian past.

Conclusion

Confucius in East Asia Today

Confucianism not only has a long history in East Asia, but still plays a role in the region today. Students once again commit Confucian teachings to memory in Chinese public schools and universities. Confucian symbols flutter in the breeze everywhere that the South Korean flag flies. In the wake of national disaster and decline, Japanese politicians rebuke the youth of their country for abandoning Confucian values. The Vietnamese government promotes Confucian festivals as both sources of tourist income and proof of its moral legitimacy. These four examples of Confucius' living legacy in contemporary East Asia all point to the central role of the state in extending the life of Confucian traditions into modernity and beyond. Therein lies the complicated nature of Confucianism's modern dilemma as an East Asian ideology. Just as there is more than one nation comprising contemporary East Asia, there is more than one Confucianism at work in East Asian societies. As in the past, current East Asian regimes look to Confucianism as a source of state authority. As they face the future, East Asian communities can find in Confucianism ways of being both modern and non-Western. And in the troubled present, East Asian individuals once again are turning to Confucianism as a resource for personal morality. These three varieties of Confucianism—state, regional, and personal—do not necessarily work with each other, and may even work against each other in certain situations, because these different ways of being Confucian entail different relationships with the state.

Since the mid-twentieth century, the East Asian region has enjoyed relatively greater political stability than was the case during the preceding one hundred and fifty years. Despite various challenges and disruptions, the continuity of state power in China, South Korea, Japan, and Việt Nam seems assured for the near future, at least. And as these regional powers exercise their considerable economic influence, they present a culturally if not politically unified alternative to the global dominance of the West, especially the United States. The recent endorsement of Confucian

Figure C.1. Nguyễn Phú Trọng (b. 1944), General Secretary of the Vietnamese Communist Party. Source: Wikimedia Commons, Presidential Press and Information Office, https://upload.wikimedia.org/wikipedia/commons/0/01/ Nguyen_Phu_Trong_3.jpg.

ideas, institutions, and practices by modern Chinese and Vietnamese governments after a century or more of anti-Confucian campaigns has rehabilitated the figure of Confucius as a symbol of East Asian political power, cultural prestige, and social and spiritual values. Values identified by contemporary East Asian states as "Confucian"—such as the need for compromise and the importance of social harmony—are identified more broadly as "Asian" by non-East Asian states such as Indonesia, Singapore, and Thailand. This convergence between "Confucian" and "Asian" values as state values promotes a "regionalism [that]… is constituted largely as a state discourse that reinforces state identity" and helps insulate "Confucian"—or "Asian"—identified governments from both domestic and foreign criticism on issues of human rights.[1] In this context, being "Confucian" is a way to build solidarity with other Asian nations while underlining fundamental differences between Asia and the West.

At the same time, just as the close identification of Confucianism with failing East Asian imperial regimes led to the rejection of Confucianism as oppressive and obsolete by nineteenth- and twentieth-century reformers and rebel movements, the increasingly intimate relationship between Confucianism and contemporary East Asian states may lead future generations of Chinese, Koreans, Japanese, and Vietnamese to rise up against both political institutions and Confucianism as an institutional ideology. During America's war of independence against Great Britain, the slogan "no bishop, no king" was used to communicate the tight links between authoritarian religious institutions (i.e., the Church of England) and authoritarian political institutions (i.e., the British monarchy). Those who question the legitimacy of Communist regimes in China and Việt Nam, Japan's post-World War Two constitution, or policies in Seoul or Pyongyang one day may cry out "no Confucius, no Chairman" (or the equivalent office).

At the regional level, the revival of Confucianism in contemporary East Asia can be understood as a response to globalization—the disappearance of national and regional borders due to the free flow of capital, ideas, and trade across cultures and communities. Prior to the end of the Cold War in the early 1990s, the globe often was divided up by Westerners into three "worlds": the First World (i.e., the West and its allies), the Second World (i.e., the Soviet bloc), and the Third World (i.e., developing nations aligned with neither the West nor the Soviets). Within the East Asian region, Japan, South Korea, Taiwan, and the European colonies of Hong Kong and Macau were tightly linked with the West, while China, North Korea, and Việt Nam were loosely associated with the Soviet Union because of shared Communist ideology. In the aftermath of the Soviet bloc's implosion, the process of globalization appeared to be a vehicle for increasing "First World" dominance of the planet by promoting Western-identified values as liberating, democratic, and cosmopolitan. More than ever before, to be "modern" was equated by many, especially triumphant "First World" thinkers, with being Western, and pro-democracy and economic reform movements in East Asian countries seemed to lend credibility to this view.

In response, some thinkers in East Asia and elsewhere began to re-conceive what it meant to be "modern" in post-Cold War terms. Must economic success and technological development come at the cost of abandoning East Asian traditions for Western values? Today, many in China, South Korea, Japan, and Việt Nam do not think so. By allowing contemporary East Asians to be both East Asian and modern at the same time, a revitalized and updated Confucianism provides an alternative model of globalization in which non-Western identities and institutions can coexist with economic, industrial, and even political institutions adapted from the West. As early as some twenty years ago, some observers predicted that the revival of Confucianism in East Asia would take the form of an anti-globalization movement.[2] Confucianism's utility as an instrument of East Asian cultural, political, and spiritual resistance against hegemonic Western values may assure its future in a region where Confucianism has been subject to criticism since the nineteenth century.

And unlike discourses on Hinduism or Islam in South and Southeast Asia, the East Asian conversation about Confucianism as an alternative form of modernity has been taking place largely among those empowered to make key economic and political decisions in the region.[3] However, the promotion of Confucianism as the basis for an East Asian regional identity may undermine the authority of individual East Asian states. This could happen if the authoritarian side of Confucianism embraced by some East Asian regimes is challenged by the principled dissent and social advocacy championed by Confucian heroes across East Asian cultural traditions. In the name of Confucianism as an East Asian regional value system, individuals and communities in China, Korea, Japan, and Việt Nam might rise up against their nominally Confucian governments.

Finally, the revival of Confucianism as a resource for personal spiritual development and benchmark for moral integrity in contemporary East Asia presents both opportunity and danger for East Asian states. Although members of various East Asian societies may define the causes of the crisis differently, the notion that moral and spiritual development have not kept pace with economic development is common across the region. China's rapidly growing income inequality, alongside its looming demographic crisis due to its lopsided ratios between old and young and male and female, have prompted its government to de-emphasize economic growth in favor of a renewed focus on social justice—a goal that is as Confucian as it is Marxist, according to Xi Jinping.[4] On the streets of Seoul, many elderly people may be found collecting scraps of cardboard for resale in order to survive, even as South Korea counts itself among the world's top ten economies.[5] The closing ceremonies of the 2020 Olympic Games held in Tokyo, delayed by one year due to COVID-19 concerns, were unusually somber, including reflections on the losses and uncertainties of life in the pandemic era and featuring a quiet parade of dim lanterns surrounding a single dancer clad in a green-and-brown tree costume while a narrator intoned, "Even if the outer layer is no longer alive, the trunk continues to live on and strengthen its centuries-old connection to the earth and land in which its roots stretch deep."[6] And the Vietnamese government struggles to contain the excesses and mitigate the social costs of their country's rapid economic development by cracking down on corruption and crime, depicting their elderly leader as "a noble man, sent by the spirits to purify the system."[7] Commentators in all four nations increasingly are calling for a return to Confucian values as a means of addressing these crises, and certainly Confucianism is a tradition that speaks eloquently to issues of moral rectitude and social responsibility.

Figure C.2. Video capture of Wang Wanze and his filial two-year-old son, whose dramatic assistance of his wheelchair-using father made him a viral sensation across Chinese social media in mid-2022.
Source: https://www.sixthtone.com/DailyTones/26638?cid=1010884.

But while it seems clear that a revived Confucianism can address the social crises that plague contemporary East Asia, it is not evident that reading the *Analects* or practicing ancestor worship will fulfill all of the spiritual needs of individual East Asians, especially when that sector of the religious market has been cornered for centuries by Buddhism and Daoism, with Christianity and new religious movements having made inroads more recently.[8] Moreover, Buddhist and Daoist traditions in modern East Asia, like their pre-modern counterparts, often promote Confucian ideas, institutions, and practices under their own umbrellas, making it less likely that contemporary East Asians will perceive Confucianism as uniquely suited to their spiritual needs. Lastly, even if the embrace of Confucianism as a personal spiritual resource once again becomes widespread among East Asians, the tradition runs the risk of becoming a depoliticized self-help ideology that privileges the therapeutic growth of individuals over witness to social justice or confrontation of official corruption, much as

Figure C.3. Hollow tree trunk decorated with tree-shaped arrangement of *omikuji* (fortune-telling paper strips), Japan. Source: Wikimedia Commons, Cyril Bèle, https://upload.wikimedia.org/wikipedia/commons/a/a9/Omikuji_tree_%28124087014%29.jpg.

some have accused Buddhism and Christianity of doing.[9] If Confucianism should become merely another way for modern East Asians to feel good about themselves amidst rapid economic and social change, then not only will important elements of Confucian tradition have been lost, but the tradition as a whole will be in danger of modernizing and commodifying itself to the point of irrelevance. *Analects* 4:16 contrasts the Confucian gentleman who understands righteousness (*yi*) with the "petty person" who understands only profit (*li*). It is difficult to reconcile this emphasis on virtue that transcends personal benefit with the kind of twenty-first-century self-help Confucianism promoted by bestselling Chinese author and media personality Yu Dan, whose *Yu Dan Lunyu xinde* (*Yu Dan's Insights into the Analects*) sold more than 10 million copies (in both official and pirated editions) within a year of its publication in 2006.[10] Yu's popularized version of Confucius teaches contemporary Chinese:

> how to attain spiritual happiness, adjust... daily routines and find [one's] place in modern life... [and] emphasize the positive things in their lives, not the negative things...[11]

Figure C.4. Statue of P.C. Chang (Zhang Pengchun, 1892–1957), Confucian-influenced principal author of the 1948 Universal Declaration of Human Rights, at Nankai University, Tianjin, China. Source: https://commons.wikimedia.org/wiki/ File:P.C._Chang%27s_Statue.png.

The type of Confucianism that sells in China and elsewhere in East Asia today may not be the type of Confucianism that is capable of challenging abuses of state power, holding rulers accountable to ethical standards, or any of the other forms of moral witness for which Confucianism rightly has taken credit over the past two and half thousand years.

What then lies ahead for Confucius in East Asia? Just as Confucianism has been a multifaceted phenomenon in East Asia's past, it is probable that the legacy of Confucius in the future East Asia will be not one, but rather many Confucianisms. Confucianism has proven useful to countless East Asian regimes, and now shows signs of being valuable to East Asian governments in a post-colonial, post-Cold War, post-modern age. In the past, Confucianism served as a kind of cultural glue that held the diverse peoples of East Asia together. Today, concerned citizens from Seoul to Sapporo and from Harbin to Hanoi share a Confucian vocabulary for identifying and addressing what is wrong with their communities and how they might be put right. It is impossible to understand the heroic, prophetic, and scholastic traditions of East Asia without reference to Confucianism, and the tradition still offers ways of expressing resistance, vision, and spiritual depth to those facing the challenges of life in contemporary East Asia. The fact that Confucianism as a state ideology, Confucianism as a regional identity, and Confucianism as a personal morality do not always work in tandem with one another does not spell the end of Confucianism as a living tradition. Rather, it is this very complexity and interdependence of Confucian ideas, institutions, and practices that most likely assures Confucianism of a future in East Asia.

NOTES

INTRODUCTION

[1] See *Socrates, Buddha, Confucius, Jesus: The Paradigmatic Individuals* (New York: Harcourt, Brace & World, 1962).

CHAPTER 1

[1] All translations from Chinese texts are adapted by the author from James Legge, trans., *The Chinese Classics* (Hong Kong: Hong Kong University Press, 1960), unless otherwise indicated.

[2] English translations of the twenty-four traditional exemplar tales may be found online at http://www.ruf.rice.edu/~asia/24ParagonsFilialPiety.html.

[3] See http://www.sacred-texts.com/journals/oc/inm.htm.

[4] "After Passing the Examination (A.D. 800)," trans. Arthur Waley, *Chinese Poems* (Mineola, NY: Dover, 2000), 120.

[5] "[Excerpts from] *Luxuriant Gems of the Spring and Autumn Annals* (*Chunqiu Fanlu*)," trans. Sarah A. Queen, in *Sources of Chinese Tradition, Vol. 1: From Earliest Times to 1600*, 2nd ed., eds. Wm. Theodore de Bary and Irene Bloom (New York: Columbia University Press, 1997), 301.

[6] Although Confucianism was known outside China well before this period, it was only in its Song and Ming dynasty formulations that Confucianism became a powerful influence on Korean, Japanese, and Vietnamese cultures. See chapters 2, 3, and 4.

[7] Adapted from A. James Gregor, "Confucianism and the Political Thought of Sun Yat-Sen," *Philosophy East & West* 31/1 (1981): 55.

[8] Josephine Ma and Jun Mai, "Death of coronavirus doctor Li Wenliang becomes catalyst for 'freedom of speech' demands in China," *South China Morning Post*, February 7, 2020, https://www.scmp.com/news/china/politics/article/3049606/coronavirus-doctors-death-becomes-catalyst-freedom-speech.

CHAPTER 2

[1] Banyan, "Confucianism has become a political punchbag in South Korea," *The Economist*, January 2, 2021, https://www.economist.com/asia/2021/01/02/confucianism-has-become-a-political-punchbag-in-south-korea. See also the "Confucian-Land" website at https://www.confucianland.com.

[2] "Traditional academy in S. Korea teaches right way to live," *People's Daily Online*, 20 September 2011, http://english.people.com.cn/90782/7600574.html.

[3] Hyung Il Pai, *Constructing 'Korean' Origins: A Critical Review of Archaeology, Historiography, and Racial Myth in Korean State-Formation Theories* (Cambridge, MA: Harvard University Asia Center, 2000), 188-189.

[4] See "Confucianism and Chinese Society" in ch. 1.

[5] "Letter to Sŏng Hon," trans. Michael Kalton, in Peter H. Lee and Wm. Theodore de Bary, eds., *Sources of Korean Tradition, Volume One: From Early Times through the Sixteenth Century* (New York: Columbia University Press, 1997), 375, 377.

[6] Quoted in Wai-ming Ng, "The I Ching in Late-Chosŏn Thought," *Korean Studies* 24 (2000): 60.

[7] See Don Baker, "Religious Diversity in Korea," *Education About Asia* 25:1 (Spring 2020): 5–10, and Franklin D. Rausch and Haeseong Park, "Christianity in Korea," *Education About Asia* 25:1 (Spring 2020): 12–18.

CHAPTER 3

[1] Eiichi Miyashiro, "Oldest writing about teachings of Confucius found in Japan," *Asahi Shimbun*, September 27, 2020, https://www.asahi.com/ajw/articles/13765362.

[2] Shunsuke Abe, "Top court: Free rent to Confucian temple in Naha is unconstitutional," *Asahi Shimbun*, February 25, 2021, https://www.asahi.com/ajw/articles/14219626.

[3] See Angela Schottenhammer, "Introduction," in *The East Asian maritime world 1400–1800: Its Fabrics of Power and Dynamics of Exchanges*, ed. Angela Schottenhammer (Wiesbaden: Harrassowitz, 2007), xiii, and George H. Kerr, *Okinawa: The History of an Island People* (Boston: Tuttle Publishing, 2000), 194, 221.

[4] Sakiko Shiraishi, "Japan court finds same-sex marriage ban unconstitutional," BBC News, March 17, 2021, https://www.bbc.com/news/world-asia-56425002.

[5] "The Seventeen-Article Constitution of Prince Shōtoku," trans. W. G. Aston and Wm. Theodore de Bary, in Wm. Theodore de Bary, et al, eds., *Sources of*

Japanese Tradition, Volume One: From Earliest Times to 1600, 2nd ed. (New York: Columbia University Press, 2001), 51, 53–54.

[6] "Preface to Kojiki, 712 A.D.," trans. Donald L. Philippi, in David J. Lu, ed., *Japan: A Documentary History, Volume I: The Dawn of History to the Late Tokugawa Period* (Armonk, NY, and London: M. E. Sharpe, 1997), 37.

[7] "Emperor Jinmu" and "Nintoku: Rule of Benevolence," trans. W. G. Aston, in Wm. Theodore de Bary, et al, eds., *Sources of Japanese Tradition, Volume One: From Earliest Times to 1600*, 2nd ed. (New York: Columbia University Press, 2001), 72–73, 75.

[8] "The Mendicant's Speech" and "A School of Arts and Sciences," trans. Yoshito S. Hakeda, in *ibid.*, 161, 171. Note that Kūkai does not mention Shintō at all, which indicates the lack of a concept of *kami* worship as a separate or distinct religious tradition at this time.

[9] "Injunctions for Peasants, c. 1619," in David J. Lu, ed., *Japan: A Documentary History, Volume I: The Dawn of History to the Late Tokugawa Period* (Armonk, NY, and London: M. E. Sharpe, 1997), 212–213.

[10] See "Confucianism and Chinese Society" in ch.1 and "Confucianism and Korean Self-Cultivation" in ch. 2.

[11] Quoted in Richard Bowring, "Fujiwara Seika and the 'Great Learning,'" *Monumenta Nipponica* 61/4 (Winter 2006): 446.

[12] On *Hanxue* and *kaozheng xue*, see "Confucianism and the Chinese State" in ch. 1.

[13] "The Divine Light in the Mind," in Ryusaku Tsunoda, et al, eds., *Sources of Japanese Tradition, Volume I*, 1st ed. (New York: Columbia University Press, 1958), 373.

[14] *Musui's Story: The Autobiography of a Tokugawa Samurai*, trans. Teruko Craig (Tucson: University of Arizona Press, 1988), 156–157.

[15] Frank Gibney, "The Real Asian Miracle," *New York Times*, July 11, 1999, http://www.nytimes.com/books/99/07/11/reviews/990711.11gibneyt.html.

CHAPTER 4

[1] Sebastian Strangio, "Vietnam Formulates Nationwide Code of Conduct for Social Media," *The Diplomat*, June 21, 2021, https://thediplomat.com/2021/06/vietnam-formulates-nationwide-code-of-conduct-for-social-media/.

[2] Sue Wootton, "Heart of Hanoi beating strong," *Otago Daily Times*, 6 March 2012, http://www.odt.co.nz/lifestyle/travel/200181/heart-hanoi-beating-strong.

[3] Some Vietnamese sources claim a much more ancient history for these early civilizations.

[4] See "The Origins of Confucianism in Korea" in ch. 2 and "The Origins of Confucianism in Japan" in ch. 3.

[5] Quoted in Nguyen Ngoc Huy, "The Confucian Incursion into Vietnam," in Walter H. Slote and George A. DeVos, eds., *Confucianism and the Family* (Albany: State University of New York Press, 1998), 94.

[6] The Duke of Zhou was a leader of China's Western Zhou dynasty (1045–771 BCE) and one of Confucius' spiritual heroes; see "The Origins of Confucianism in China" in ch. 1. On Zhu Xi and "Neo-Confucianism," see "Confucianism and Chinese Society" in ch. 1.

[7] Quoted in Stephen B. Young, "The Orthodox Chinese Confucian Social Paradigm versus Vietnamese Individualism," in Walter H. Slote and George A. DeVos, eds., *Confucianism and the Family* (Albany: State University of New York Press, 1998), 145–146.

[8] Nguyen Khac Vien, "Confucianism and Marxism in Vietnam," in Nguyen, *Tradition and Revolution in Vietnam* (Berkeley, CA: Indochina Resource Center, 1974), 17.

[9] Quoted in Shawn Frederick McHale, *Print and Power: Confucianism, Communism, and Buddhism in the Making of Modern Vietnam* (Honolulu: University of Hawai'i Press, 2004), 91.

[10] Quoted in Liam C. Kelley, "'Confucianism' in Vietnam: A State of the Field Essay," *Journal of Vietnamese Studies* 1/1–2 (February–August 2006): 336.

[11] Quoted in Wai-ming Ng, "*Yijing* Scholarship in Late-Nguyen Vietnam: A Study of Le Van Ngu's *Chu Dich Cuu Nguyen* (*An Investigation of the Origins of the Yijing*, 1916)," http://hmongstudies.com/NgPaper2003.pdf.

[12] Ibid.

[13] Quoted in David G. Marr, *Vietnamese Anticolonialism, 1885–1925* (Berkeley: University of California Press, 1970), 63.

[14] "Vietnam, 1975–1980: Reflections on a Revolution," *Contemporary Southeast Asia* 2/2 (September 1980): 95.

CONCLUSION

[1] Jessie P. H. Poon, "Regionalism in the Asia Pacific: Is Geography Destiny?," *Area* 33/3 (September 2001): 257.

[2] Gilbert Rozman, "Can Confucianism Survive in an Age of Universalism and Globalization?" *Pacific Affairs* 75/1 (Spring 2002): 36.

[3] Arif Dirlik, "Confucius in the Borderlands: Global Capitalism and the Reinvention of Confucianism," *boundary* 2 22/3 (Autumn 1995): 271.

[4] Karen Yeung, "China's economy downshifts to slower growth path as focus turns to social equality, national safety," *South China Morning Post*, August 3, 2021, https://www.scmp.com/economy/china-economy/article/3143651/chinas-economy-downshifts-slower-growth-path-focus-turns.

[5] Shin Ji-hye, "Why do old people pick up cardboard in Seoul?," *The Korea Herald*, February 25, 2021, http://www.koreaherald.com/view.php?ud=20210225000695.

[6] Merrit Kennedy, "Closing Ceremony Caps Off A Dramatic, Bittersweet And Ultimately Uplifting Olympics," National Public Radio, August 8, 2021, https://www.npr.org/sections/tokyo-olympics-live-updates/2021/08/08/1025880512/closing-ceremony-caps-off-a-dramatic-bittersweet-and-ultimately-uplifting-olympics.

[7] James Pearson, "Nguyen Phu Trong, Vietnam's anti-corruption czar, crowned party chief again," Reuters, January 31, 2021, https://www.reuters.com/article/us-vietnam-politics-trong/nguyen-phu-trong-vietnams-anti-corruption-czar-crowned-party-chief-again-idUSKBN2A006T.

[8] Peter Berger, "Is Confucianism a Religion?," *The American Interest*, February 15, 2012, http://blogs.the-american-interest.com/berger/2012/02/15/is-confucianism-a-religion/.

[9] See Gil Hizi, "Help yourself China – The rise of self-help culture and its unique Chinese features," *Ministry of Tofu*, April 27, 2012, http://www.ministryoftofu.com/2012/04/help-yourself-china-the-rise-of-self-help-culture-and-its-unique-chinese-features/; David Loy, "How Buddhist is Modern Buddhism?," *Tricycle*, Spring 2012, http://www.tricycle.com/reviews/how-buddhist-modern-buddhism; and Bong Rin Ro, "Bankrupting the Prosperity Gospel," *Christianity Today*, November 16, 1998, http://www.ctlibrary.com/ct/1998/november16/8td058.html.

[10] See Sheila Melvin, "Modern Gloss on China's Golden Age," *New York Times*, September 3, 2007, http://www.nytimes.com/2007/09/03/arts/03stud.html.

[11] Ibid.

Glossary

Analects (Chinese *Lunyu*): "collected sayings" of Confucius and his disciples, compiled after the death of Confucius in 479 BCE and before the end of the Han dynasty in 220 CE.

Âu Lạc: ancient Vietnamese state that flourished between the seventh and second centuries BCE.

Buddhism: religious tradition originating in fifth-century BCE India that teaches salvation through renunciation of individual desire and ego.

Christianity: religious tradition originating in first-century CE Palestine that teaches salvation through faith in humanity's redemption by one incarnate God.

communism: ideology originating in nineteenth-century CE Europe that teaches social transformation through collective ownership of the means of production by the working class.

Đại Việt: independent Vietnamese state founded in 938 and ruled by the Lý dynasty.

Dao: Chinese term that literally means "Way," used throughout East Asia as a byword for natural law, spiritual truth, or religion in general.

Daoism: religious tradition originating in second-century CE China that teaches salvation through the cultivation of individual harmony with cosmic processes and natural patterns.

Fuxi: legendary Chinese cultural hero who is credited with the invention of writing.

globalization: disappearance of national and regional borders due to the free flow of capital, ideas, and trade across cultures and communities.

jing: Chinese term that means "classic" or "scripture," used to designate texts as authoritative or canonical in Buddhism, Confucianism, and Daoism.

kami: Japanese term that means "deity" or "spirit," used to refer to supernatural forces, local gods, or exemplary human beings worshiped in Shintō traditions.

karma: Sanskrit term that means "action," used in Buddhism to describe both the moral value and supernatural consequences of intentional human activity.

Laozi: legendary Chinese sage credited with authorship of a text bearing his name, also known as *Daodejing*; later regarded as a Daoist deity.

Liji (*Record of Ritual*): Han dynasty text regarded as a Confucian scripture.

Mencius (372–289 BCE): earliest interpreter of Confucius's teachings whose views most shaped Confucian orthodoxy, credited with authorship of the text bearing his name.

Nam Việt (204–111 BCE): Chinese vassal state in what is now southeastern China and northern Việt Nam.

Neo-Confucianism: general term used to describe various Confucian revival movements that spread from China to the rest of East Asia beginning in the ninth century CE.

Paekche: ancient state in southwestern Korea that flourished during the first seven centuries CE.

Shakyamuni (sixth–fifth centuries BCE): name by which the historical Buddha, who lived in ancient India, is known; *see* Buddhism.

Shijing (*Classic of Poetry*): collection of early Chinese poems associated with Western Zhou dynasty culture, later regarded as a canonical Confucian text.

Shintō: Japanese term used to describe ideas, institutions, and practices associated with the worship of *kami.*

Shujing (*Classic of Documents*): collection of early Chinese chronicles associated with Western Zhou dynasty culture, later regarded as a canonical Confucian text.

Silk Roads: term used to describe the network of trade routes linking premodern Asia, Africa, and Europe.

Sino-Japanese War: term used to describe two conflicts between China and Japan, the first from 1894 to 1895 and the second from 1937 to 1945.

T'aegŭk: "the Great Ultimate," Korean term used to describe the cosmic interaction of *yin* and *yang.*

Tian: Chinese term that means "Heaven" or "Sky," used by Confucius to describe the supernatural source of cosmic moral order originally worshiped as a deity by Western Zhou dynasty rulers.

Văn Lang: ancient Vietnamese state that flourished from antiquity until the third century BCE.

xiao: Chinese term that means "filial piety" or reverence owed to one's elders, a paramount Confucian virtue.

Xiaojing (*Classic of Filial Piety*): early Confucian document later regarded as a canonical text.

Yijing (*Classic of Changes*): early Chinese divination manual and commentaries associated with Western Zhou dynasty culture, later regarded as a canonical Confucian text.

yin and **yang:** paired Chinese terms used to describe the opposite but complementary forces seen as underlying all cosmic phenomena; analogous to female/male, dark/light, and so on.

Zhongyong (*Doctrine of the Mean*): early Confucian text regarded as a canonical text by neo-Confucian thinkers.

Suggestions for Further Reading

Confucianism: General

Ames, Roger T., and Peter D. Hershock, eds. *Confucianisms for a Changing World Cultural Order*. Honolulu: University of Hawai'i Press, 2017.

Angle, Stephen C. Sagehood: *The Contemporary Significance of Neo-Confucian Philosophy*. New York: Oxford University Press, 2012.

Bell, Daniel A. and Hahm Chaibong, eds., *Confucianism for the Modern World*. Cambridge University Press, 2003.

Berthrong, John H. *Transformations of the Confucian Way*. Boulder: Westview Press, 1998.

Clarke, J. J. *Oriental Enlightenment: The Encounter Between Asian and Western Thought*. London and New York: Routledge, 1997.

Elman, Benjamin A., Duncan, John B., and Ooms, Herman, eds. *Rethinking Confucianism: Past and Present in China, Japan, Korea, and Vietnam*. Los Angeles: UCLA Asian Pacific Monograph Series, 2002.

Ko, Dorothy, JaHyun Kim Haboush, and Joan R. Piggott, eds. *Women and Confucian Cultures in Premodern China, Korea, and Japan*. Berkeley: University of California Press, 2003.

Lee, Ming-Huei. *Confucianism: Its Roots and Global Significance*. Ed. David Jones. Honolulu: University of Hawai'i Press, 2017.

Li, Chenyang, ed. *The Sage and the Second Sex: Confucianism, Ethics, and Gender*. Chicago: Open Court, 2000.

Rozman, Gilbert. "Can Confucianism Survive in an Age of Universalism and Globalization?" *Pacific Affairs* 75/1 (Spring 2002): 11–37.

Rozman, Gilbert, ed. *The East Asian Region: Confucian Heritage and its Modern Adaptation*. Princeton: Princeton University Press, 1991.

Slote, Walter H., and George A. DeVos, eds. *Confucianism and the Family*. Albany: State University of New York Press, 1998.

Son, Bui Ngoc. *Confucian Constitutionalism in East Asia*. Basingstoke: Taylor and Francis Ltd., 2016.

Taylor, Rodney L. "The Religious Character of the Confucian Tradition." *Philosophy East and West* 48/1 (January 1998): 80–107.

Taylor, Rodney Leon. *The Religious Dimensions of Confucianism*. Albany: State University of New York Press, 1990.

Tu, Wei-ming and Mary Evelyn Tucker, eds. *Confucian Spirituality*. 2 vols. New York: Crossroad, 2003-04.

Yao, Xinzhong, ed. *Encyclopedia of Confucianism*. 2 vols. London and New York: RoutledgeCurzon, 2003.

Zhang, Weibin. *Confucianism and Modernization: Industrialization and Democratization of the Confucian Regions*. New York: St. Martin's Press, 1999.

CONFUCIANISM: CHINA

Adler, Joseph A., trans. *Introduction to the Study of the Classic of Change (I-hsüeh ch'i-meng)*. Provo, UT: Global Scholarly Publications, 2002.

Billioud, Sébastien, ed. *The Varieties of Confucian Experience: Documenting a Grassroots Revival of Tradition*. Leiden and Boston: Brill, 2018.

Bresciani, Umberto. *Reinventing Confucianism: The New Confucian Movement*. Taipei, Taiwan: The Taipei Ricci Institute for Chinese Studies, 2001.

Chan, Alan K., ed. *Mencius: Contexts and Interpretations*. Honolulu: University of Hawai'i Press, 2002.

Chan, Wing-tsit, ed. *A Source Book in Chinese Philosophy*. Princeton: Princeton University Press, 1963.

Chan, Wing-tsit, trans. *Instructions for Practical Living and Other Neo-Confucian Writings*. New York: Columbia University Press, 1963.

Chan, Wing-tsit, trans. *Reflections on Things at Hand*. New York: Columbia University Press, 1967.

Chang, Carsun. *The Development of Neo-Confucian Thought*. 2 vols. New York: Bookman Associates, 1957–962.

Chen, Chun. *Neo-Confucian Terms Explained: The Pei-hsi tzu-I by Ch'en Ch'un (1159–1223)*. Trans. and ed. Wing-tsit Chan. New York: Columbia University Press, 1986.

Ch'eng, Chung-ying. *New Dimensions of Confucian and Neo-Confucian Philosophy*. Albany: State University of New York Press, 1991.

Ching, Julia. *To Acquire Wisdom: The Way of Wang Yang-ming*. New York: Columbia University Press, 1976.

Ching, Julia. *The Religious Thought of Chu Hsi*. New York: Oxford University Press, 2000.

Csikszentmihalyi, Mark, ed. *Readings in Han Chinese Thought*. Indianapolis and Cambridge: Hackett Publishing Company, 2006.

De Bary, Wm. Theodore, and Irene Bloom, eds. *Sources of Chinese Tradition, Vol. I: From Earliest Times to 1600*. 2nd ed. New York: Columbia University Press, 1997.

De Bary, Wm. Theodore, and Richard Lufrano, eds. *Sources of Chinese Tradition, Vol. II: From 1600 through the Twentieth Century*. 2nd ed. New York: Columbia University Press, 2000.

Ebrey, Patricia Buckley, trans. *Chu Hsi's Family Rituals: A Twelfth-Century Chinese Manual for the Performance of Cappings, Weddings, Funerals, and Ancestral Rites*. Princeton: Princeton University Press, 1991.

Eno, Robert. *The Confucian Creation of Heaven*. Albany: State University of New York Press, 1990.

Fingarette, Herbert. *Confucius—The Secular as Sacred*. New York: Harper Torchbooks, 1972.

Foster, Robert W. "Understanding the Ethical Universe of Neo-Confucianism." In Jeffrey L. Richey, ed., *Teaching Confucianism* (New York: Oxford University Press, 2008), 107–155.

Gardner, Daniel K., trans. *The Four Books: The Basic Teachings of the Later Confucian Tradition*. Indianapolis: Hackett, 2007.

Gardner, Daniel K. *Zhu Xi's Reading of the Analects: Canon, Commentary, and the Classical Tradition*. New York: Columbia University Press, 2003.

Gardner, Daniel K., trans. *Learning to Be a Sage: Selections from the Conversations of Master Chu, Arranged Topically*. Berkeley: University of California Press, 1990.

Graham, A. C. *Disputers of the Tao: Philosophical Argument in Ancient China*. La Salle, IL: Open Court, 1989.

Hammond, Kenneth J., and Jeffrey L. Richey, eds. *The Sage Returns: Confucian Revival in Contemporary China*. Albany: State University of New York Press, 2015.

Hartman, Charles. *Han Yü and the T'ang Search for Unity*. Princeton: Princeton University Press, 1986.

Ivanhoe, Philip J. *Confucian Moral Self Cultivation*. 2nd ed. Indianapolis: Hackett Publishing Company, 2000.

Ivanhoe, Philip J. *Ethics in the Confucian Tradition: The Thought of Mengzi and Wang Yangming*. 2nd ed. Indianapolis: Hackett, 2002.

Jensen, Lionel M. *Manufacturing Confucianism: Chinese Traditions & Universal Civilization*. Durham: Duke University Press, 1997.

Kline, T.C. III, and Philip J. Ivanhoe, eds. *Virtue, Nature, and Moral Agency in the Xunzi*. Indianapolis: Hackett, 2000.

Knapp, Keith Nathaniel. *Selfless Offspring: Filial Children and Social Order in Early Medieval China*. Honolulu: University of Hawai'i Press, 2005.

Knoblock, John. *Xunzi: A Translation and Study of the Complete Works*. 3 vols. Stanford: Stanford University Press, 1988–1990.

Ko, Dorothy. *Teachers of the Inner Chambers: Women and Culture in Seventeenth-Century China*. Stanford: Stanford University Press, 1994.

Liu, Shu-hsien. *Essentials of Contemporary Neo-Confucian Philosophy*. Westport, CT and London: Praeger, 2003.

Liu, Shu-hsien. *Understanding Confucian Philosophy: Classical and Sung-Ming*. Westport, CT: Praeger, 1998.

Makeham, John. *Lost Soul: "Confucianism" in Contemporary Chinese Academic Discourse.* Cambridge: Harvard University Press, 2008.

Makeham, John. *Transmitters and Creators: Chinese Commentators and Commentaries on the Analects.* Cambridge: Harvard University Asia Center, 2003.

Nylan, Michael. *The Five 'Confucian' Classics.* New Haven and London: Yale University Press, 2001.

Slingerland, Edward, trans. *The Essential Analects: Selected Passages with Traditional Commentary.* Indianapolis: Hackett, 2006.

Smith, Richard J. *Fathoming the Cosmos and Ordering the World: The Yijing (I Ching, or Classic of Changes) and Its Evolution in China.* Charlottesville: University of Virginia Press, 2008.

Sun, Anna. *Confucianism as a World Religion: Contested Histories and Contemporary Realities.* Princeton: Princeton University Press, 2013.

Tu, Wei-ming. *Centrality and Commonality: An Essay on Confucian Religiousness.* Albany: State University of New York Press, 1989.

Van Norden, Bryan W., ed. *Confucius and the Analects: New Essays.* New York: Oxford University Press, 2002.

Van Norden, Bryan W., trans. *Mengzi: With Selections from Traditional Commentaries.* Indianapolis: Hackett, 2008.

Wilson, Thomas A., ed. *On Sacred Grounds: Culture, Society, Politics, and the Formation of the Cult of Confucius.* Cambridge: Harvard University Asia Center, 2002.

CONFUCIANISM: KOREA

Baker, Don, "Religious Diversity in Korea," *Education About Asia* 25:1 (Spring 2020): 5–10.

Ch'oe, Yŏngho, Peter H. Lee, and Wm. Theodore de Bary, eds. *Sources of Korean Tradition, Volume II: From the Sixteenth to the Twentieth Centuries.* New York: Columbia University Press, 2000.

Chung, Edward Y. J. *The Korean Neo-Confucianism of Yi T'oegye and Yi Yulgok: A Reappraisal of the "Four-Seven Thesis" and Its Practical Implications for Self-Cultivation.* Albany: State University of New York Press, 1995.

de Bary, Wm. Theodore, and JaHyun Kim Haboush, eds. *The Rise of Neo-Confucianism in Korea*. New York: Columbia University Press, 1985.

Deuchler, Martina. *The Confucian Transformation of Korea: A Study of Society and Ideology*. Cambridge: Council on East Asian Studies, Harvard University, 1992.

Kalton, Michael C., trans. *To Become a Sage: The Ten Diagrams on Sage Learning by Yi T'oegye*. New York: Columbia University Press, 1988.

Kim, Anselm K., ed. *Korean Religions in Relation: Buddhism, Confucianism, Christianity*. Albany: State University of New York Press, 2016.

Kim, Youngmin and Michael J. Pettid, eds. *Women and Confucianism in Choson Korea: New Perspectives*. Albany: State University of New York Press, 2011.

Lancaster, Lewis, and Richard Payne, eds. *Religion and Society in Korea*. Berkeley: Institute for East Asian Studies, University of California, 1998.

Lee, Peter H., and Wm. Theodore de Bary, eds. *Sources of Korean Tradition, Volume I: From Early Times through the Sixteenth Century*. New York: Columbia University Press, 1997.

Phillips, Earl H., and Eui-young Yu, eds. *Religions in Korea: Beliefs and Cultural Values*. Los Angeles: Center for Korean-American and Korean Studies, California State University, Los Angeles, 1982.

Rausch Franklin D. and Haeseong Park, "Christianity in Korea," *Education About Asia* 25:1 (Spring 2020): 12–18.

Sleziak, Tomasz. "The Role of Confucianism in Contemporary South Korean Society." *Annual of Oriental Studies* - Rocznik Orientalistyczny LXVI (2013): 27–46.

CONFUCIANISM: JAPAN

Bellah, Robert. *Tokugawa Religion: The Cultural Roots of Modern Japan*. New York: The Free Press, 1985.

Boot, Willem Jan. *The Adoption and Adaptation of Neo-Confucianism in Japan: The Role of Fujiwara Seika and Hayashi Razan*. Leiden: Lectura, 1982.

De Bary, Wm. Theodore, Carol Gluck, and Arthur I. Tiedemann, eds. *Sources of Japanese Tradition, Volume Two: 1600 to 2000*, 2nd ed. New York: Columbia University Press, 2006.

De Bary, Wm. Theodore, Donald Keene, George Tanabe, and Paul Varley, eds. *Sources of Japanese Tradition, Volume One: From Earliest Times to 1600*, 2nd ed. New York: Columbia University Press, 2001.

Dore, Ronald. *Education in Tokugawa Japan*. Ann Arbor: University of Michigan Center for Japanese Studies, 1984.

Heisig, James W., Thomas P. Kasulis, and John C. Maraldo, eds. *Japanese Philosophy: A Sourcebook*. Honolulu: University of Hawai'i Press, 2011.

Kumazawa, Banzan. *Governing the Realm and Bringing Peace to All below Heaven*. Trans. John A. Tucker. Cambridge: Cambridge University Press, 2020.

Lu, David J., ed., *Japan: A Documentary History, Volume I: The Dawn of History to the Late Tokugawa Period*. Armonk, NY, and London: M. E. Sharpe, 1997.

Lu, David J., ed., *Japan: A Documentary History, Volume II: The Late Tokugawa Period to the Present*. Armonk, NY, and London: M. E. Sharpe, 1997.

Maruyama, Masao. *Studies in the Intellectual History of Tokugawa Japan*. Trans. Mikiso Hane. Princeton: Princeton University Press, 1974.

McMullen, James. *The Worship of Confucius in Japan*. Leiden and Boston: Brill, 2020.

Najita, Tetsuo. *Japanese Thought in the Tokugawa Period, 1600–1868: Methods and Metaphors*. Chicago: University of Chicago Press, 1978.

Najita, Tetsuo. *Visions of Virtue in Tokugawa Japan: The Kaitokudô Merchant Academy of Osaka*. Chicago: University of Chicago Press, 1987.

Nosco, Peter, ed. *Confucianism and Tokugawa Culture*. Princeton: Princeton University Press, 1984.

Paramore, Kiri. *Japanese Confucianism: A Cultural History*. Cambridge: Cambridge University Press, 2016.

Reitan, Richard M. *Making a Moral Society: Ethics and the State in Meiji Japan*. Honolulu: University of Hawai'i Press, 2010.

Tucker, Mary Evelyn. *Moral and Spiritual Cultivation in Japanese Neo-Confucianism: The Life and Thought of Kaibara Ekken (1630–1714)*. Albany: State University of New York Press, 1989.

CONFUCIANISM: VIỆT NAM

Bui, Ngoc Son. "The Confucian Foundation of Hồ Chí Minh's Vision of Government / 胡志明政治思想中的儒學基礎. *Journal of Oriental Studies* 46/1 (2013): 35–59.

Cường, Nguyễn Tuấn. "The Promotion of Confucianism in South Vietnam (1955–1975) and the Role of Nguyễn Đăng Thục as a New Confucian Scholar." *Journal of Vietnamese Studies* 10/4 (2015): 30–81.

Dutton, George Edson, Jayne Susan Werne, and John K Whitmore, eds. *Sources of Vietnamese Tradition*. New York: Columbia University Press, 2012.

Kelley, Liam C. "'Confucianism' in Vietnam: A State of the Field Essay." *Journal of Vietnamese Studies* 1/1-2 (February–August 2006): 314–370.

Ly, Tung Hieu. "Confucian Influences on Vietnamese Culture." *Vietnam Social Sciences* 5/169 (2015): 71–81.

McHale, Shawn Frederick. *Print and Power: Confucianism, Communism, and Buddhism in the Making of Modern Vietnam*. Honolulu: University of Hawai'i Press, 2004.

Nguyễn, Khắc Viện. *Tradition and Revolution in Vietnam*. Berkeley: Indochina Resource Center, 1974.

Nguyễn, Quang Điển, ed. *Confucianism in Vietnam*. Ho Chi Minh City: Vietnam National University, Ho Chi Minh City Publishing House, 2002.

Nguyễn, Xuan Thu. *Vietnamese Studies in a Multicultural World*. Melbourne: Vietnamese Language and Culture Publications, 1994.

Tran, Anh Q. *Gods, Heroes, and Ancestors: An Interreligious Encounter in Eighteenth-Century Vietnam*. New York: Oxford University Press, 2018.

Tran, Nhung Tuyet. *Familial Properties: Gender, State, and Society in Early Modern Vietnam, 1463–1778*. Honolulu: University of Hawai'i Press, 2018.

Woodside, Alexander B. *Community and Revolution in Modern Vietnam*. Boston: Houghton Mifflin, 1976.

CPSIA information can be obtained
at www.ICGtesting.com
Printed in the USA
JSHW061812191222
35156JS00001B/67